This is a case study of an important 19th-century business. *Carriages from New Haven* traces the emergence of the industry against a background of the general commercial development of New Haven and its surroundings and of the development of transportation throughout the country. The story is continued, through the growth of the manufacturing industry to its achievement of a position of national and international prominence until its decline and eventual demise early in the 20th Century.

This is the first extensive survey of the business to be published. It is based on a survey of a wide variety of sources and is illustrated with unusual photographs and drawings not readily available. A chapter is devoted to the leaders of the industry and there is careful examination of the contents and nature of the carriage company catalogues. City directories and newspapers have been made use of where appropriate.

D1566376

CARRIAGES FROM NEW HAVEN
New Haven's Nineteenth-Century Carriage Industry

1. James Brewster's carriage factory at the foot of Wooster Street from Storer's *New Haven as It Is*, 1845.

Carriages from New Haven

New Haven's Nineteenth-Century Carriage Industry

BY
RICHARD HEGEL

ARCHON BOOKS 1974

Library of Congress Cataloging in Publication Data

Hegel, Richard, 1927-
   Carriages from New Haven.

   Bibliography: p.
   1. Carriage industry—New Haven—History. I. Title.
HD9999.C33U483   338.4'7'6886   74-4032
ISBN 0-208-01434-9

© 1974 by Richard Hegel
First published 1974 as an Archon Book,
an imprint of The Shoe String Press, Inc.,
Hamden, Connecticut 06514

Printed in the United States of America

Once again for Linda

Contents

Illustrations

Preface

There has existed no extensive survey of New Haven's nineteenth-century carriage industry. While it receives considerable attention in Atwater's *History of The City of New Haven* (1887), the treatment is essentially only a presentation of names, dates, and locations, with an emphasis on the mid-century period. New Haven city directories, whose publication began in 1840, will also help ascertain with some degree of accuracy the names, places of business, and years of existence of local companies. Rollin G. Osterweis's comprehensive *Three Centuries of New Haven, 1638-1938* (1953), gives the industry scholarly notice although, and quite properly, only as one of the many factors significant in the development of modern New Haven. Here ends published information on the subject.

Carriages from New Haven traces the emergence of the New Haven industry in the early nineteenth century against a background of the general industrial and business development of the area, outlining its growth to both national and international prominence. A chapter is devoted to the leaders of the industry. There is an examination of New Haven carriage company catalogues, manuscript material, and appropriate newspaper articles. The work concludes with the twilight of the industry at the turn of the century. It is hoped this detailed inspection of a local nineteenth-century industry will provide serviceable material for a better understanding of New Haven of the twentieth century.

The illustrations used are not easily available elsewhere.

New Haven, Connecticut   RICHARD HEGEL
1974

CARRIAGES FROM NEW HAVEN
New Haven's Nineteenth-Century Carriage Industry

The Development
of Early American
Transportation   I

For all practical purposes there were no coaches or carriages used in the New World for nearly two centuries after
the discovery of the American continent. Horseback and
wagon provided the means of travel by land. Prior to the
Revolution, the colonists looked toward Europe and the West
Indies for their trade, and inland transportation did not seem
pressing. Once independence was gained a far greater need
developed for some domestic transportation system.[1]

In 1645 the tavern-keeper at New Haven was allotted
twenty acres of land for the pasture of travellers' horses. In
1647 a trip by horse carrying mail from New York to Boston
first made a reality of the Boston Post Road. (The Revolution
caused its original name, the Kings Highway, to become un-
popular.) For many years this route was only a vague trail
through the forest.[2] In 1717 the General Assembly of Connecticut granted permission to Captain John Munson of New
Haven to establish a wagon line to Hartford.[3] By 1770 highways of sorts led from New Haven in nearly every direction,
many of them post-roads. After 1772 stagecoaches began to
carry both passengers and mail between Boston and New
York, and in 1784 the first regularly scheduled line of mail
stagecoaches was established between the two cities.[4]
Tavern-to-tavern was one method of stating stagecoach dis-

tances. In New Haven the Andrews tavern, near the north-west corner of the Green, was a popular coaching inn. At the beginning of the nineteenth century the stagecoach office in New Haven on Church Street south of Chapel was the important changing point for travellers. With the advent of the steamboat the terminus for stage lines returned to an earlier location near the waterfront.[5] With few exceptions only farm wagons and comparatively crude carts were built in the American colonies until the mid-eighteenth century. Sleds provided a popular and customary form of winter transportation.[6] Not many coaches or carriages were in use until after independence had been declared. A private carriage was a rarity.[7]

Generally, with the exception of turnpikes, the older roads in the northeastern part of the United States were never planned but were natural outgrowths of cartways or pedestrian paths. By far the greater number of highways consisted of little more than paths or trails through the otherwise unbroken wilderness. Most people did not own carriages or wagons and as a consequence much of the population had no direct need for roads.[8] It was difficult to get towns to cooperate in maintaining roads and they suffered neglect and were in constant disrepair. One problem was the building and upkeep of bridges. Ferries were used instead of bridges in some places. As a result of the usually poor condition of Connecticut roads many travellers from Boston to New York went by land to Newport or New London and took ship to Oyster Bay and proceeded through Long Island. Some went all the way by water. But since boats were always at the mercy of tides and winds, numbers of travellers did not wish to risk a long delay and so perforce took the trip entirely by land.[9]

To understand more fully how road systems developed it is necessary to know the general locations of the various townships. Position, of course, determined the number and direction of the highways.[10] Roads were naturally first laid out to serve the inhabitants of a particular town, passing from farm to farm as well as to and from the center of town. Next came roads from town to town. At and after the close of the revolutionary war the increase in the volume of traffic and the wide general need for improved transportation stimulated considerable road building. Improvement internally within the United States and consequent expansion and economic development is considered to have begun substantially with the formation of bridge and turnpike companies toward the end of the eighteenth century.[11] During the years 1790-1810 great dissatisfaction with existing highway conditions led to the construction of many turnpike roads, but in actuality these offered little improvement over existing road conditions.[12]

In Connecticut, initially New Haven and then Hartford began construction of turnpikes in order to bring the country trade into town. A Hartford and New Haven Turnpike Company was incorporated in 1798 and the New Haven and Milford Turnpike was built in 1802.[13] At the turn of the century the carriage building trade was in its infancy but the improvement of old roads and the construction of new ones was helping to create a demand for light pleasure vehicles.[14] Readily available supplies of lumber and an abundance of iron and steel enabled carriages of increasing serviceability to be assembled. The carriage industry developed almost simultaneously in many areas, with Wilmington, Newark, New Haven, Bridgeport, Philadelphia and New York among the early centers. Carriage building also developed in a minor way in many smaller towns throughout New England.[15]

The era of stagecoach travel in New England lasted until about 1840 or shortly thereafter—stagecoaching in England also reached its zenith at approximately the same time—when the steamship and the railroad came into their own. While steam railroads did away with the main stage lines, many local lines continued to operate throughout the horse and buggy age. A stagecoach carrying mails, the Hartford Stage running through Fair Haven, operated from New Haven as late as 1869.[16] During the 1820s and 1830s steamboats had produced marked changes in travel patterns and travel by water remained popular in varying degrees throughout the century. The New Haven Steamboat Company, the first steamboat company to provide regular service from New Haven, received its charter in 1822. It maintained an established service many years before the advent of the railroads.[17]

The New Haven area shared in the development of canals. The early nineteenth-century Farmington Canal was designed to link New Haven with the interior parts of the state. Ultimately it became the route of a railroad. The first railroad charters in Connecticut were granted by the General Assembly in 1832. The rail line between New Haven and Hartford was opened in 1840 and was extended to Springfield in 1844. In 1848-1849 rail traffic was established from New Haven to Plainfield and beyond, from New Haven to New York, and from Bridgeport up the Naugatuck Valley. In 1852 the New Haven and New London Railroad opened. The New Haven, Middletown and Willimantic Railroad began operation in 1870 and the New Haven and Derby Railroad the following year. During the post-Civil War period the various railroads serving New Haven were combined into the New York, New Haven and Hartford Railroad.[18]

It was first believed that the construction of railroads would cause a decline in the carriage building trade. But to the contrary, the new wealth created by the railroads stimulated rather than depressed the industry.[19] There was a revolution in all aspects of land transportation as the railroad systems were more widely developed and used. By 1864 railway mail service had been established.[20] Railroads, of course, increased the accessibility of many towns. No stations existed during the early days of rail travel. Railroads, following the example of the stage and canal companies, provided no special buildings to take care of freight or passengers, but allowed inns and hotels to serve as the terminal points for travellers, as had the earlier companies.[21]

The Civil War acted as a stimulus to the carriage building industry. The government's need for wagons was urgent, and quite a number of new wagon building firms sprang up. The quick populating of the west after the War added further opportunities for the trade.[22]

Street railways with their horse-cars began being used in the country's larger cities about 1850. Horse-car lines were an early method of encouraging urban expansion, for the extension of street railways encouraged the private development of outlying land, since they made it possible to build homes one or two miles from the center of town. They also increased the volume of downtown business by bringing people to the central areas.[23] By the 1870s every significant city had horse-car lines which carried workers to and from work or to the centers of shopping. These horse-cars were in turn banished by cars run by electricity as swiftly as the stagecoaches had been cast aside by steam railroads. The first major electric trolley system was installed in Richmond, Virginia, during 1887. There followed a rapid changeover to electricity in many parts of the country. Eventually the three-phase electrical distribution systems introduced in 1894 made intercity trolley systems practicable. The electric trolley with its comparative speed helped to diminish congestion in the cities, while at the same time increasing the momentum of a city's growth.[24]

The earliest horse-car railroad in New Haven was the Fair Haven and Westville, chartered in 1860. In 1865 the New Haven and West Haven and also the New Haven and Centerville were incorporated. Other lines soon followed. The horse-trolley bound together New Haven's various neighborhoods and made the central district accessible to the suburban dweller. In 1893 the first electric trolley wires were raised in New Haven.[25]

The decade of the 1890s was one of vicissitudes for the carriage and wagon industry. A general economic depression occurred throughout the nation in the middle of the period. Additionally, the bicycle was becoming a significant method of personal transportation, in turn to be replaced increasingly after 1900 by the motorcar. In 1899 in the United States 312 factories made bicycles, and the demand exceeded the supply.[26] The first workable gasoline motorcar appeared in 1893; in 1900 twelve American automobile manufacturers produced a total of 4,192 vehicles.[27]

At one time a trolley network provided a means of intercity travel throughout most of the United States. The rapid rise of the interurban railway system did not occur until the end of the nineteenth century. The interurban, evolving from the urban electric street railway, was an American phenomenon, bridging the gap between the horse and buggy and the automobile. In the twentieth century it became a casualty of the motor car and highway construction.[28]

In the New Haven area the interurban provided competition to the New Haven Railroad, which consequently acquired the competing lines and then operated them in a manner complementary to its own services. The first bus placed in use in New Haven was seen in 1900, belonging to the Orange Street Auto Line.[29] From ship and wagon and carriage to train and motor car and bus—the story of local transportation in the nineteenth century.

The Growth of Manufacturing in the New Haven Area During the Late Eighteenth and Early Nineteenth Centuries

Immediately after the signing of the Treaty of Paris in 1783 ending the War of Independence, British merchants proceeded to flood the American market with goods as best they could. Little domestic manufacturing of importance existed at the time, in part as a result of the long period of British rule when the mother country supplied manufactured items, at the same time restricting American manufacturing. During the Revolution the necessary preoccupation with making gunpowder contributed to the slow development of local manufacturing. The break from the mother country quite naturally caused a shortage of goods of all sorts. In New Haven specifically "there was an enormous demand for everything."[1]

As one method of stimulating enterprise New Haven hastened to pardon the Tories. Their business experience and capital were needed. At a town meeting held in New Haven on March 3, 1784, the following motion was acted upon affirmatively:

> *Voted*, That Pierpont Edwards, John Whiting, David Austin, David Atwater, Sam Huggins, James Hillhouse, Jonathan Ingersoll and Jonathan Dickerman be a committee to consider the propriety and expediency of admitting as inhabitants of

this town persons who in the course of the late war adhered to
the cause of Great Britain against the United States, and are of
fair characters, and will be good and useful members of society
and faithful citizens of this State, and that said committee
report to this meeting.

This motion promptly led to a report that paved the way for
the readmission of those who had supported the British to the
town's business life.[2] It was at this time James Hillhouse became New Haven's most prominent business promoter as well
as its philanthropic benefactor. He "had a great love for New
Haven" and seemed a part of every new or constructive pro-
ject that was undertaken.[3] New Haven inventors, and also
many throughout the country, displayed little activity until
after the War, when American industry was at last freed from
British restrictions. From this period forward New Haven became the home of prominent inventors, men who contributed
greatly to the life of the city—Charles Goodyear and Eli Whitney were outstanding examples.[4] Quite soon there was evidence of the beginning of new manufacturing in New Haven,
an activity encouraged by the state legislature. A monopoly
for the refining and manufacture of loaf sugar was granted to
a local group headed by Elias Shipman. The woolen cloth
manufacturing concern of Atwater and Lyon received a five-
year tax abatement. James Hillhouse, in association with
several other New Haven men, in 1785 was voted a license to
manufacture copper coins. This occupation continued until
the Federal Constitution prohibited state coinage.[5]
"In 1784 the manufactories of New Haven were apparently
a paper mill and a blacksmith shop." The incorporation in
1784 of New Haven as a city was promoted by those who believed that the action would provide New Haven, by increasing its authority, with greater power for economic development; increased municipal authority supposedly would offer
a stimulus to trade and manufacturing. For many the city's
incorporation was primarily a plan to promote business. To

further promote general business the New Haven Chamber of Commerce was founded in 1794.[6]

The shift in emphasis at the end of the eighteenth and at the beginning of the nineteenth centuries from agriculture to manufacturing had far-reaching effects. In New Haven as elsewhere banks rather than country merchants became the money lenders and insurance companies came into being. Distribution and transportation methods improved rather substantially. In the towns a laboring class of some size first appeared. Early nineteenth-century restrictions on international trade such as Non-Importation, the Embargo, and Non-Intercourse followed by the blockade during the War of 1812 further manifested the need for American manufacturing. Under such restrictions capital that had once flowed into shipping was released for other business activities. One result of the Embargo Act, for example, was the creation of a demand for domestic wool. The demand encouraged General David Humphreys, of revolutionary fame, to cultivate merino sheepraising. In turn this product stimulated the establishment of woolen factories at Seymour and New Haven. Presidents Jefferson and Madison both obtained suits cut from cloth manufactured by Humphreys at Seymour. Additionally local shops engaged in the making of cotton goods. Other businesses in New Haven were producing buttons, clocks, tinware, wagons and carriages. At the beginning of the nineteenth century New Haven was thus experiencing its own industrial revolution.[7]

Industrialization was favorably aided in New Haven, as it was in other parts of the county, by the existence of a combination of human and natural resources coupled with social forces conducive to industrial growth.[8] A prominent and increasing spirit of manufacturing prevailed in New Haven and throughout Connecticut. The opening in 1798 of Eli Whitney's gun factory at Hamden, where interchangeable parts were used in the manufacture of firearms, was probably the most important single event in the economy of the New

Haven area at the turn of the century. In 1793 Whitney had invented the cotton gin. Some thirty-eight years later John Warner Barber gave the following summation of New Haven's carriage industry, which had emerged and flourished as part of the expanding manufacturing prosperity:

> There are within the city limits twelve coach making establishments; and it is estimated that the value of carriages manufactured at present, will amount to about half a million dollars annually. There are also four coach-spring and step manufactories, and five plating establishments.[9]

It need hardly be added that the products of the developing New England urban craftsmen were generally more skillfully designed and manufactured with greater care and precision than earlier rural counterparts had been,[10] in itself a spurt to the business economy.

The Rise
of New Haven's
Carriage Industry   III

New Haven's earliest known carriage maker, John Cook, with a business dating from 1794, headed what was also Connecticut's first carriage manufacturing concern. The vehicle he offered was two-wheeled. Four-wheeled carriages were not introduced until about 1812, with construction of the first four-wheeled carriage in the state generally being attributed to Maltby Fowler of Northford.[1] Shortly after 1800 several small carriage-making shops already existed in New Haven. Captain Jonathan Mix invented the elliptical steel spring used in most carriages, patented in 1807, a considerable improvement over previous arrangements. During the early years of the nineteenth century carriage building gradually became a significant factor among New Haven's industrial activities,[2] although carriages did not come into popular use until well into the century because of their relatively high cost and also because of the poor conditions of roads.

> Carriages and Wagons were not very common until the commencement of the present [nineteenth] century. Some of the aristocracy or "Notables," rode in Chaises or *Chairs,* as they were called. In 1762, there were only four in New Haven. Boys were obliged to carry the *grist* to mill upon the backs of horses,

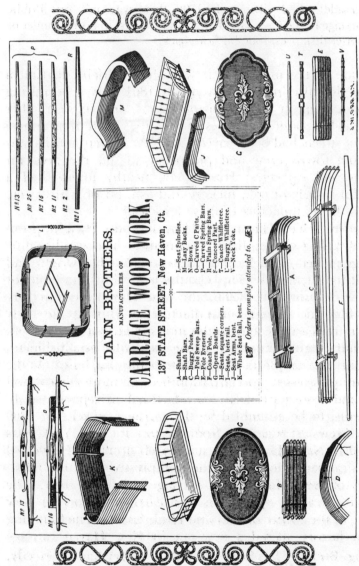

2. Dann Brothers advertisement from *G. & D. Cook & Co.'s Illustrated Catalogue of Carriages and Special Business Advertiser*, 1860.

and sometimes had a great deal of trouble, especially when the bags were not well *balanced*. Wives and daughters rode upon sidesaddles and pillions. In 1798, there was only one Public Carriage in the City. Gentlemen and Ladies, in going longer or shorter distances, rode on horseback.[3]

As late as the mid-1840s it was often difficult to find a carriage for hire in New Haven.[4] By 1861 only a beginning had been made in macadamizing streets, and six years after the Civil War only four miles of the city's more than ninety miles of streets had been paved.[5] As New Haven and its surrounding towns grew and prospered so did the need for wagons and carriages. Fortunately, nearby forests had a plentiful supply of oak, hickory and ash, all of which were used in the manufacture of these vehicles.[6]

A survey of New Haven in 1811 by Timothy Dwight, president of Yale College, listed twenty-nine blacksmiths, nine carriage makers, four harness makers, one wheelwright and about fifty carpenters.[7] This was the work force available for the new industry. By 1860-61 the New Haven city directory listed fifty-one carriage manufacturers.[8] During the early stages of the carriage and wagon industry almost all the work of manufacturing was done at the particular establishment, with only certain pieces of hardware being purchased. As the industry progressed, specialization became more evident and more and more parts were manufactured in separate establishments, to be assembled by the carriage maker.[9] In 1809 James Brewster, traveling from Boston to New York, was delayed in New Haven by a stagecoach accident. He visited Cook's carriage shop and became impressed with the possibilities of New Haven as a carriage-building center. The following year he opened his own carriage factory in New Haven, at the corner of Elm and High Streets. The founding of this factory started a new era in New Haven carriage making. Brewster has been referred to, somewhat incorrectly, as the father of the local industry. He brought good workmen to New Haven and strove to increase their sense of responsibility. He believed in contributing to higher standards of workmanship by paying adequate wages in cash, not in trade as had often been the custom. In addition Brewster took somewhat paternalistic measures to raise the workmen's mental capacity and moral standards.[10]

The economic recession following the War of 1812 slowed activity. The use of luxuries had to be curtailed and the fashion came about of using light wagons and one-horse carriages. Brewster capitalized on this vogue created of necessity and concentrated on improving light vehicles. His buggies, phaetons, and rockaways became very popular. In 1832 Brewster constructed a new and larger factory at the foot of Wooster Street, not far from the Pavilion Hotel, which soon became the best known local carriage manufactory.[11] After further establishing himself as a producer of improved vehicles for ordinary consumption, Brewster turned his talents to the construction of fine vehicles of outstanding style, carriages equalling the best of those manufactured in England.

> He was soon producing buggies, phaetons, victorias, and other forms of equipage for a large market, especially in the South. A visitor to the Charleston or New Orleans race track, in this period, could see long lines of New Haven-made carriages, their pannels bearing the heraldic devices of proud owners moving toward the grandstand.[12]

A federal government report in 1832 indicated that the capital employed in New Haven coach making amounted to $41,000, representing investment in grounds, buildings, and machinery. Yearly New Haven production was 800 coaches or similar vehicles with a value of $221,000. Employed in the local industry were 217 men working a ten-hour day at an average wage of one dollar and twelve to one dollar and thirteen cents per day. At the time three quarters of the city's coach production was exported by means of coastwise shipping.[13]

It is reported that in 1840 twelve carriage factories were located in New Haven with total production valued at $234.000.[14] Between 1840 and the beginning of the Civil War a period of great activity and prosperity for the city's carriage industry existed. It was during this time New Haven carriage manufacturers established their significant and substantial trade in the southern states, a domestic market mainly accessible by sea.[15] New Haven between 1845 and 1855 also produced some early hand-operated fire engines.[16] In 1851 a German immigrant, Gustavus Haussknecht, obtained patents for carriage improvements—an enthusiasm for the carriage trade seemed communicable to newcomers.[17]

Because of the wide publicity early steamboats and railroads received the stationary steam engine was not particularly noticed by people of the time. Nevertheless, prior to the Civil War, the stationary steam engine was important to Connecticut industry and its significance has not been generally recognized.[18] Throughout most of New England the introduction of steam power dates from early in the nineteenth century, although it did not come into extensive use until after the midcentury. By 1838 there were forty-seven stationary steam engines in operation in Connecticut. Eleven New Haven manufacturing firms reported that they employed them. In the same year there were 317 such engines operating throughout New England.[19] In 1838 the Collins & Lawrence coach manufacturing company of New Haven reported having used an eight-horsepower steam engine for ten years for sawing, turning, and grinding. By the mid-1840s six steam engine manufacturing establishments were located in Connecticut. With the increased introduction and acceptance of steam power after 1840 the pace of the carriage manufacturing business in New Haven increased.[20]

George T. Newhall of New Haven became impressed with the large scale application of steam power as it had been used in Providence. His introduction in 1855 of steam machinery on a large scale marked another milestone in the history of the New Haven carriage industry. Not everyone was favorably impressed with his use of steam driven equipment:

> . . . his creditors became anxiously filled with the idea that he was doomed to insolvency, or the retreat for the insane. The success of the enterprise was, however, soon apparent.

By the time of the Civil War most factories in the New Haven area had steam power and machinery.[21] The importation of coal in the nineteenth century first from England and later in substantial quantities from Pennsylvania, naturally played an important part in the industrial expansion of New Haven, permitting the wide use of steam power.[22]

The first New Haven carriage manufacturer to apply mass production methods was G. & D. Cook & Co. In the late fifties they began systematizing work in their shops and increased production from one carriage a day to ten. An assembly line similar to that of a modern automobile plant was used enabling this then remarkable output of one vehicle an hour. The company employed 300 men in its twenty-four departments.[23]

During the financial crisis of 1857 the area carriage industry remained strong. Over 7,000 vehicles valued at $1,613,150 were manufactured in that year, chiefly for the southern market. By 1860 there were nearly fifty manufacturers of carriages and their accessories in New Haven and the city had now become one of the world's most important centers of carriage production. In 1859 vehicle production at New Haven had been greater than that in any of the states but Connecticut, exclusive of the city, New York, and Pennsylvania.[24]

In the 1860 national election Lincoln received 3,140 votes from New Haveners, the Northern Democrat Douglas 1,331, but 1,681 votes went to Breckenridge, the Southern Democrat. Breckenridge's popularity is quite probably traceable to the

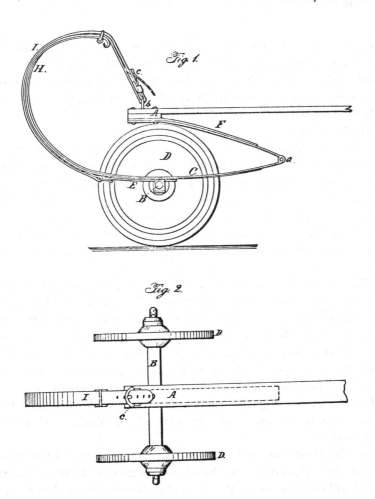

3. Gustavus Haussknecht, *Carriage Spring*, Letters Patent, No. 8221,
July 15, 1851.

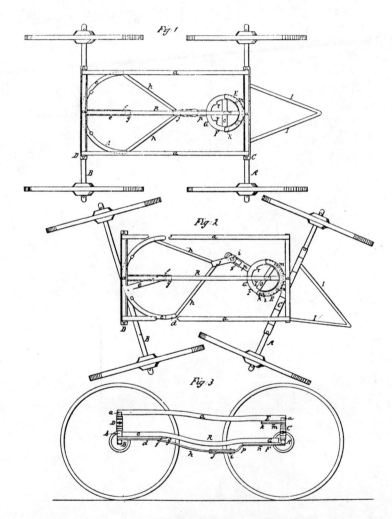

Fig. 1

Fig. 2

Fig. 3

4. Gustavus Haussknecht, *Carriage,* Letters Patent, No. 8588, December 16, 1851.

importance of the southern market to the New Haven carriage industry.

> Many New Haven industrialists and merchants supported the attempts at compromise between North and South, which were advanced between the election of November, 1860, and the inauguration of March, 1861.[25]

In many respects New York City had by 1860 extended its business and commercial influence over the New Haven area. The local carriage industry was more or less dependent upon distribution agents and credit sources in New York and through contacts such as these the industry was assisted in reaching many of its southern markets. New Haven carriage manufacturing was economically hard hit by the start of the Civil War because of its heavy dependence on the South; accounts outstanding in the Confederacy became uncollectible.[26] While the South had been the mainstay of the trade, carriages were also exported to the Caribbean, to South America, and to the Pacific Islands.[27] By 1863, however, local business had improved to the point where New Haven manufacturers were producing more luxury vehicles than they had in 1860. Many companies during the war, previously financially distressed because of the loss of southern customers, found that due to the great number of orders for army wagons they could not meet their civilian demands.[28]

> The extensive Carriage Factory of G. & D. Cook & Co. is at present a real bee-hive for industry—but not exactly in the peaceful character of its origin. Instead of the light and tasteful pleasure vehicles, for which it was a few months ago so famous, it is now fashioning large bars of iron and heavy oak, into ponderous gun-carriages; but the thorough finish of the latter, is fully equal to the former. Indeed, better work of the kind was probably, never seen in any country.—In other large rooms, are scores of girls and men, working on knapsacks and haversacks; in others, long platoons of shoemakers at work on

army shoes; and from top to bottom of this spacious factory, every foot of room is occupied—and all goes on with the regularity and order which is proverbial of the establishment.[29]

And while the New Haven carriage industry concentrated on Civil War production and the making of such articles as gun carriages, many thoughtful residents realized that the southern market would not survive the war, certainly as it had existed, and that new channels of trade must be sought.[30]

During the third quarter of the century a significant change in carriage manufacturing methods developed, brought about by a division of the industry into many related but separate segments, each of which specialized in the making of a particular part.

> Thus we find manufacturers of axles, bodies and hardware, which are again subdivided into such articles as springs, wheels, steps, tops, poles, and trimmings. This division of work, by its natural tendency to produce skilled workmen for every part, has also tended to system, superior workmanship, beauty of finish, and cheapness; and has thus created for New Haven carriages an enviable reputation throughout the world.[31]

The New Haven Wheel Co., for example, was for many years the largest company in the United States engaged exclusively in the production of wheels. About half of its work was for export. As carriage parts became interchangeable the cost of carriage manufacture declined.[32]

In response to the demand for skilled craftsmen in the carriage industry there came to New Haven in addition to American workers, English, Scotch, Welsh, and German. Negroes found little employment in this local industry.[33] New Haven workingmen generally tended to live near their places of employment. With the exception of the Whitney Armory development in Hamden, company housing for employees was not a factor in nineteenth-century New Haven. As the city's manufacturing capacity accelerated thousands of units of workers' housing became closely packed around the hundreds of factories. Most of the buildings in which the workers found homes were built by speculators who had no direct connection with the factory owners. The area surrounding the Brewster Carriage factory on East Street, known as the old carriage manufacturing district, always had a particularly heavy concentration both of carriage manufacturing sites and workers' dwellings.[34]

5. James Brewster from Atwater's *History of The City of New Haven,*
1887.

Men
Who Made
the Industry IV

JAMES BREWSTER,
THE SYMBOL OF
THE NEW HAVEN CARRIAGE INDUSTRY

James Brewster was born in Preston, Connecticut, on August 6, 1788, and died in New Haven on November 22, 1866. His birth predated by only a few years John Cook's establishment of his carriage factory in New Haven in 1794. Brewster, the second of eight children, was one of the seventh generation in a direct descent from Elder William Brewster, who had come to this country in 1620 on the *Mayflower*. James's mother lived to an advanced age, but the death of his father when James was quite young, coupled with the family's limited financial means, made it necessary that he soon follow a trade. Brewster had only a limited formal education. In 1804 he was apprenticed to learn the carriage-making trade from Colonel Charles Chapman of Northampton, Massachusetts. He refused an interest in his employer's firm on completion of his apprenticeship since he preferred to go into business for himself.

In 1810 Brewster married Mary Hequembourg of Hartford. The Brewsters had six children, one of whom died in infancy. Two of his sons, James B. Brewster and Henry Brewster, became prominent in New York City carriage manufacturing firms bearing the Brewster name. The third son, Joseph Brewster, became a minister.

A stagecoach breakdown in 1809 introduced James Brewster to New Haven, where the following year he opened a small carriage-making business. As in many other New England locations the factor of chance had played an important part in influencing a local industry. Brewster's shop, located in a one-story building at the corner of Elm and High Streets, proved successful. Subsequently he moved to Elm and Park Streets and when this factory in turn became too small he secured a larger location on Orange Street. Brewster became known for his production method of dividing the work of the factory into different departments. His custom of paying workers in cash instead of with orders for goods was evidence of his concern for them. Brewster, a strong advocate of temperance, also showed his concern by barring intoxicating drink from the factory even though liquors were customarily used in most local shops with the consent of the employer. On January 28, 1857, he spoke to a group of young men on the subject of what he conceived to be the poison of life:

> Now, my young friends, I must put some stress upon this part of my address. To understand the physical laws of our being, is one of the main sources of our happiness; and to you its study and appreciation is peculiary [sic] appropriate. Yours is the springtime of life; your usefulness to yourselves, to your parents, and to community, depends mainly upon the decisions you make in regard to the exercise of your reason and judgment, and the use of the physical laws of your nature. I presume you anticipate the application. If you pervert your powers by idleness—by intemperance, either in eating or drinking—or by encroaching upon the proper hours of sleep, you cannot expect to enjoy health. Where there is not health, there is not enjoyment. As you value health, therefore, cultivate all the means which promote it, and avoid everything which injures it. Be industrious and temperate in all things—shun all unnaturally exciting causes—as the greatest bane, avoid all intoxicating

drinks—and, whatever your situation in life may be, LEARN TO
CONFORM TO CIRCUMSTANCES.

James Brewster and his wife Mary as well have been
described as possessing industry, frugality, skill, integrity,
and enterprise. Brewster possessed a great respect for religion
and in many ways endeavored to educate his employees in it,
stressing particularly that the Bible should be read. Alto-
gether his various efforts on behalf of workingmen attracted a
superior class of mechanic to New Haven. He sought to build
better carriages than the English and continuously undertook
the improvement of carriage styles and made a specialty of
the better type of vehicles. Brewster was the first Northern
manufacturer in the United States to send a panelled carriage
to the South, although many such carriages had previously
been imported from England. Among his customers were
Andrew Jackson and Martin Van Buren. During 1827 Brewster opened a branch of his business in New York in association with John Lawrence as a partner, under the firm name of
Brewster and Lawrence. Brewster organized the Young
Mechanics' Institute and rented a room for meetings in the
Glebe Building located at Church and Chapel Streets. He
often delivered evening addresses on moral and practical
subjects. In response to the demand in New Haven for a city
lyceum the Franklin Institute was founded in 1831, for which
Brewster financed the renovation of a building at the corner
of Church and Crown Streets, which before its conversion had
been Morse's Hotel. The building, referred to by many as
Franklin Hall, included a lecture hall seating 300 persons and
various classrooms, as well as facilities for displaying collections in natural history, mineralogy, geology, and conchology.
Brewster early in life developed a strong sense of identity
with Benjamin Franklin. Many times he studied Franklin's
maxims for as long as an hour a day. He liked to point out that
he had refused money for a college education and by so doing
had followed Franklin's belief that a trade was preferable to a

profession. Brewster instituted a course of scientific lectures by prominent men, including many Yale professors, contributing $5,000 a year toward their cost. Charles U. Shepard described the Franklin Institute.

> The FRANKLIN INSTITUTION *has for its object to afford popular lectures, collections in several departments of natural history, and facilities for obtaining practical information relating to the application of science to the arts.* It is intended to supply the citizens of New-Haven [*sic*] with those advantages which numerous communities in this country and in Britain are now enjoying from associations for the popular discussion and elucidation of science, and for the investigation of the inventions and improvements of the age.
>
> Through the enterprise of a single individual, MR. JAMES BREWSTER of this city, the institution is able to offer its advantages directly to this community, without subjecting it to that loss of time which is necessarily connected with the organization of a general society; and what is still more important without the possibility of endangering the union and vigor of useful societies already existing, against which liability its individual character is a sufficient guarantee. Its objects are more general than those of any society existing at present in our community.

In general business practice Brewster made it a policy to pay obligations and notes in full when they became due rather than to follow the prevailing custom of extending them.

In 1832 Brewster moved to a large factory at the foot of Wooster Street, an area where he acquired a total of twenty-three acres. Concurrent with the moving of the factory he assisted in developing the new neighborhood by the creation of new streets and the widening of older ones. As a result of his efforts in public improvement the area came to be known as Brewsterville. The name Brewsterville is no longer used for this area south and east of Wooster Square, but the Newhallville designation of the city's north central section, named for the carriage manufacturer George T. Newhall, still survives. Another family name of local carriage makers is probably perpetuated by Bradley Street.

Subsequent and successor Brewster firm names were Brewster and Collis; Collis and Lawrence; Lawrence, Bradley and Pardee and later William H. Bradley & Co. In 1833 together with a number of New Haven citizens Brewster obtained a charter for the construction of the railroad between New Haven and Hartford. He gave up much of his carriage business to devote full time to the building of the railroad and was elected its first president. On February 25, 1836, Brewster's carriage factory in Brewsterville burned with an estimated loss of $60,000. So as to have time to realign his financial interests he then sold the remainder of his carriage business and also resigned as president of the railroad. In 1838 he again established a carriage business, this time in association with his son, James B. Brewster.

In 1838 he helped found the New Haven Savings Bank, the area's first savings bank. He was one of the organizers in 1849 of the New Haven Water Company. In 1849 Brewster joined those supporting the construction of a new City Hall, the building of which was completed in 1862. Brewster aided in improving the New Haven Almshouse and in 1855 gave the Orphan Asylum building to the City with the municipality providing the land for the structure. At his instigation New Haven purchased its first horse-drawn steam fire engine in 1860. During the same year Brewster reduced his real estate holdings because of declining health and the heavy burden of management. His various activities did not prevent his participation in politics, although he was not as successful here as he was in his other pursuits. Brewster was defeated as the Republican candidate for mayor of New Haven in 1857.

In addition to his southern accounts Brewster had customers in South America, Cuba, and other West Indian Islands. Despite his extensive market in the South he was opposed to slavery. James F. Babcock, a biographer of Brewster, discussed Brewster's viewpoints concerning the South.

> He had extensive business relations with the South, and was always averse to slavery, and never hesitated to avow his opinions on this subject; but it was always with so much kindness and charity that he rarely offended his southern customers. On one occasion, a distinguished author, Col. Fitzhugh, of Virginia, lectured in this hall [Merchants' Exchange] in defense of slavery. He maintained that the workingmen of the North bore the same relation to capital that the slaves of the South did to their masters. The next day Mr. Brewster took the lecturer into his carriage and showed him many handsome houses, owned and occupied by New Haven mechanics; and finally they went into one of them, where neatness, order and comfort everywhere prevailed. When they came out, Mr. Brewster remarked that such was the effect of northern capital upon New Haven mechanics, "what do you think of it Mr. Fitzhugh?" "Stop, stop, Mr. Brewster," the Colonel good naturedly replied, "stop, or you will make me an abolitionist." They, of course, parted good friends.
>
> When the slave controversy culminated in war, Mr. Brewster, though advanced in years, took a decided stand in support of the old flag and the Union it represented, and his general contributions, even to the equipment of the Brewster Rifles, are well known to us all.

James Brewster's name figured prominently in the construction of business property during the pre-Civil War years. He was the "grand old man" of industrial New Haven on the eve of the war. His death in November 1866 marked to many the passing of an era and also of a phase in New Haven's pre-eminence in the carriage industry. He had done much to create the local industry which had dominated New Haven's industrial scene in the years prior to the Civil War. Yet the industry did not disappear from the area as a result of the war, even though the conflict and its aftermath brought many problems. Before his death Brewster had joined with Leverett

Candee, Edward Marble, and Henry Hooker in purchasing the firm of G. & D. Cook & Co. This firm, which in 1868 became Henry Hooker and Co., proved a success and did much to carry on the industry in new fields.

For many years Brewster's name was a hallmark for soundly designed and sturdily built carriages. He set the style in American vehicles. The growth and importance of the New Haven carriage industry was in great part due to him.

References

Account of the Golden Wedding of James and Mary Brewster, September 18, 1860 (printed at the request of their children; New Haven: Thomas J. Stafford, 1860), p. 17.

Atwater, pp. 558-559.

Babcock, p. 16.

James Brewster, *An Address Delivered at Brewster's Hall, on Wednesday Evening, Jan. 28, 1857, to the Young Men of New Haven, Ct.* (New York: Isaac J. Oliver, 1857), pp. 11-12.

Dana, p. 25.

Downing and Kinney, p. 91.

LeBlanc, pp. 61-62.

Edwin Mitchell, p. 16.

New Haven as It Is (New Haven: William Storer, 1845), pp. 14-15.

Palladium [New Haven], March 7, 1860, p. 3.

Charles U. Shepard, *Outline of the Franklin Institution of New Haven* ((?) : Baldwin and Treadway, (?)), pp. 1-2.

Stone, p. S3.

Alexander Catlin Twining Papers, New Haven Colony Historical Society, a manuscript collection. Letter of James Brewster to Alexander Catlin Twining dated March 25, 1841, Box VI, item No. 123.

John Cook,
New Haven's
Pioneer Carriage Manufacturer

John Cook was New Haven's and Connecticut's earliest carriage manufacturer. He was born at New Haven on May 23, 1757, and died there on September 8, 1835. He was the son of John Cook and his second wife, Martha Booth. John Cook's paternal grandfather was the Rev. Samuel Cook, a Trustee of Yale College from 1732 until 1746, and his paternal grandmother was a descendant of William Leete, an early Governor of Connecticut. John Cook married on May 26, 1787, Anne Lyon, the daughter of William and Elizabeth (Maltby) Lyon of New Haven. They had a son named John Howard Cook, but the exact number of their children is unknown.

John Cook established his carriage business in 1794, manufacturing what was at the time the principal carriage of the period, the two-wheeled chaise or gig. In the same year Samuel Clark was also doing business in New Haven as a carriage maker. John Cook's original place of business on Orange St. was the small shop that James Brewster visited in 1809 when the stagecoach on which Brewster had been traveling from Boston to New York stopped in New Haven for repairs. John Cook was recognized as "a man of some importance" in the community. He was an Episcopalian and belonged to the local Mechanics Society. While Cook may have been New Haven's first carriage manufacturer, his chief contribution to the local industry was no doubt the part he played in influencing Brewster to settle in New Haven and to open his own manufacturing business.

References

Atwater, p. 556.

Beals, pp. 95, 130-133.

Connecticut Journal, July 23, 1794, p. 3. (Samuel Clark advertisement)

The Daily Herald [New Haven], September 9, 1835, p. 2. (John Cook death notice)

New Haven, Connecticut: *Records of the Registrar of Vital Statistics,* Vol. 5, p. 68. (John Cook death record)

New Haven Old and New, Carriage Factories, A-E, Vol. CXXVII, New Haven Colony Historical Society, a scrapbook collection, p. 10.

Osborn, pp. 203-204.

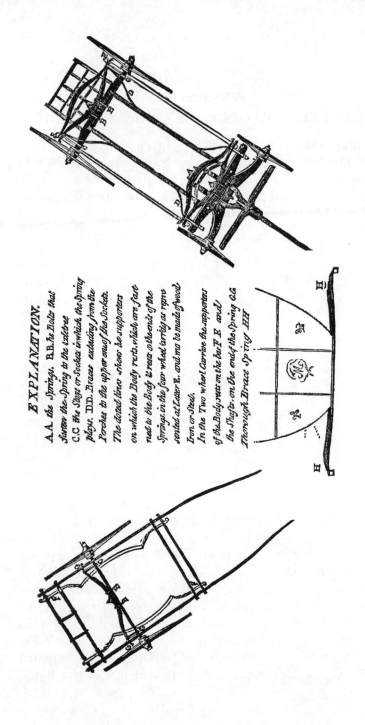

EXPLANATION.

A.A. the Springs.   B.B. the Bolts that
fasten the Spring to the axletree
C.C. the Stays or Sockets in which the Spring
plays. D.D. Braces extending from the
Porches to the upper ones of the Sockets.
The dotted lines shews the supporters
on which the Body rests, which are fast-
ned to the Body & rests on the ends of the
Springs; in the four wheel carriage as represented at Letter E. and may be made of wood
Iron, or Steel.
In the Two wheel Carriage the supporters
of the Body rests on the bar F. F. and
the Shafts on the end of the Spring G.G.
Thorough Brace Spring HH

6. Jonathan Mix's carriage suspension based on his patents of 1807 and 1808 from Blake's *Life and Patriotic Services of Jonathan Mix*, 1886.

Jonathan Mix,
Inventor of
the Elliptical Steel Carriage Spring

Jonathan Mix was born in New Haven on April 19, 1753, at his father's home located on the northwest corner of College and Elm Streets where Calhoun College now stands. He died in New York on January 18, 1817. Mix was a descendant in the fourth generation from Thomas Mix (Meekes), one of the early settlers of New Haven. The family was comfortable financially. Jonathan Mix's father, also Jonathan, married Mary Peck. Young Jonathan had two older brothers, William and John. After his mother's death his father married Patience Alling. Two sons, Eldad and Joseph, and two daughters, Mary and Elizabeth, resulted from this second marriage.

Jonathan Mix, the inventor of the elliptical steel carriage spring, married Anna Sears on August 6, 1776. They had ten children, James Peck, Elijah, Clarissa, Jonathan Marvin, Marvin Peck, Nancy Maria, Jonathan Lucis, Mary Eliza, William Augustus, Julia Ann. His first wife died on June 23, 1799. On August 5, 1800, he married Elizabeth Mary Phipps. They had one child, a daughter, Adeline Nancy. Elizabeth Mary Phipps Mix lived until 1849.

As a young man Jonathan Mix joined the New Haven Cadets in their historic march in April 1775 to Cambridge under the command of Captain Benedict Arnold. Mix returned from Massachusetts in July with a desire to serve on an armed vessel of war. Because of the lack of an opportunity, however, he joined the forces of General David Wooster and subsequently served with the rank of captain on Long Island. Mix was later ordered to Canada under Wooster's command, but was separated from the expedition after an accident on Lake Champlain. He returned to New Haven in October of 1775 and in November participated in a land raid on New York. Early in 1776 he entered the Naval Service and participated in a successful attack against New Providence in the Bahamas, as well as in several other naval actions. After naval service as a Lieutenant of Marines he was honorably discharged at his own request in February, 1777. Sometime later Mix rejoined the military forces. He served as Captain of Marines and saw service in the English Channel. When the British invaded New Haven in July 1779 Mix aided in the resistance. In 1782, a passenger on a ship outside of Delaware Bay, he was taken prisoner by the British and confined for nearly six months on the infamous Jersey Prison Ship near New York. He returned home to New Haven under parole in June 1782, broken in health and fortune.

Mix thereafter devoted himself to commercial activity in New Haven and pursued his talents as an inventor, achieving more success in the latter endeavors. Sometime in 1799-1800 he built the house on Elm St. which is now the Graduates Club.

Jonathan Mix's most significant invention was the steel axle-tree spring, or elliptic spring for carriages and other vehicles. He was the first to propose attaching a spring to the axle-tree parallel with its length, to be fastened by bolts or bands in the center. In 1807 he procured a patent for this device under the name of Main Springs for Carriages [Patent for Improvement in Main Springs for Carriages, April 18, 1807]. In 1808 he obtained a patent for Through-Brace Springs [Patent for Through-Brace Springs for Carriages, June 17, 1808]. There is a Mix family tradition that when the first carriage was provided with the new main springs he took his wife for a ride around the New Haven Green and told her that with such an invention neither she nor her children would ever be without their own coach to ride in. After disappointment in commerce in New Haven, Mix moved to New York in 1808, entering the mercantile business. He prospered for a while until the War of 1812 brought him financial troubles. During the hostilities Mix devoted time to the improvement of firearms and worked on the design of cartouch boxes and the development of a plan to carry off smoke from the fuse of cannon. As the result of these activities he found himself once more in military service and again served with distinction.

The Mix carriage spring developments made both the old-style iron coil spring and the previous leather suspension straps obsolete. Jonathan Mix, patriot and soldier, is best remembered in New Haven as an inventor and an important contributor to the impetus and success of New Haven's carriage industry. Today's Mix Avenue in Hamden perpetuates the family name.

References

Beals, p. 123.

William Phipps Blake (ed.), *A Brief Account of the Life and Patriotic Services of Jonathan Mix of New Haven Being an Autobiographical Memoir* (New Haven: Tuttle, Morehouse and Taylor, 1886), *passim.*

Rachel M. Hartley, *The History of Hamden, Connecticut, 1786-1959* (Hamden: The Shoe String Press, 1959), *passim.*

George T. Newhall,
For Whom the Newhallville Section
of the City Took Its Name

George T. Newhall was born in New Haven on Goffe Street in 1821 and died in Orange, Connecticut, in 1902, in that section which is now West Haven. Newhall's father, Merritt, married a Miss Thompson, who was a descendant of William Leete, as was John Cook. George T. Newhall was survived by three daughters, Harriet, Imogene, and J. Adele, as well as three sons, one of whom was named George T. Newhall, Jr.

George T. Newhall learned the carriage-making trade in New Haven at the Hooker and Osborne factory on Park Street. When quite a young man he entered business for himself and actively continued in the trade for over forty years. He normally did not have a partner but at one time he was in partnership with Joseph Pardee and later with Singleton Carrington. During the winter of 1849-50 Newhall acquired an old mill in New Haven located on the bank of the former Farmington Canal, now replaced by a railroad, and purchased an adjacent section of canal property. After purchasing the mill and moving his carriage business there he soon increased his working force to over 200 people.

Subsequently Newhall acquired large tracts of land in the neighborhood from Henry and Joseph Munson and from the Ives Estate. He opened streets, built a number of houses, and generally improved the property. At one time he owned over 5,000 feet of frontage on various streets. Today his name is remembered in the area's name of Newhallville. Street names like Newhall, Munson, and Thompson remind us of the neighborhood's history.

Newhall visited Providence and was impressed with the many applications of steam power he saw there. He realized steam could be used to great advantage in carriage manufacturing and in 1855 purchased a steam engine to install in his factory at Newhallville. His success with steam machinery soon became apparent. At the beginning of the Civil War almost every factory in New Haven had steam power, a significant reason, to repeat, for the success of New Haven's carriage industry. Newhall established assembly lines and so introduced mass production to what was at one time the largest carriage manufacturing factory in the world, producing a vehicle every hour. Newhall's factory also manufactured street horse-cars.

As with others, Newhall's business was mainly with the South. When the Civil War began he had $65,000 in accounts receivable on his books, all in the South, less than $4,000 of which was ever collected. Nevertheless, he clung to his business and real estate until 1872 when his financial affairs finally made an assignment necessary. After this reversal he literally began his financial life anew. Newhall went to Chicago where through a chance meeting with a former Connecticut resident he obtained employment as a book salesman. He prospered and expanded his line of publishers. In 1880, after having had considerable financial success, he returned to New Haven. He purchased property at the corner of Park and Martin (now Edgewood Avenue) Streets and there once again began a carriage business. In the middle of the last decade of the century he retired from manufacturing and purchased a farm in Orange, where he died in 1902.

References

Atwater, p. 557.

Beals, pp. 182, 192.

New Haven Register, May 31, 1902, p. 2.

Osborn, 205-206.

Palladium [New Haven], June 6, 1890, p. 4.

William Porter, "The Farmington Canal," *New Haven Colony Historical Society Journal*, Vol. XX, October, 1971, 62.

West Haven, Connecticut: *Records of the Registrar of Vital Statistics*, May 29, 1902. (George T. Newhall death record)

7. G. & D. Cook & Co. from G. & D. Cook & Co.'s Illustrated Catalogue of Carriages and Special Business Advertiser, 1860.

The Industry
Depicted through
Catalogues and Records   V

An examination of nineteenth-century New Haven carriage company manuscript material, catalogues, and related items provides a means of ascertaining how the industry viewed itself and was seen by others.

The most extensive of the catalogues reviewed is *G. & D. Cook & Co.'s Illustrated Catalogue of Carriages and Special Business Advertiser* of 1860. It contains illustrations of more than one hundred of the company's carriages showing the tremendous variety of horse drawn vehicles produced at New Haven—Buggies, Phaetons, Sporting Wagons, Barouches, Rockaways, Sulkies, Chaises, Cabriolets, Coaches, French Dog Carts, and Calashes, to mention but a few. There are also over one hundred advertisements of other firms, many from the area around New Haven. Advertisements include those from banks, hotels, schools, suppliers to carriage manufacturers, in addition to many others featuring representative products of the mid-nineteenth century. The company's pride both in itself and in New Haven is evident:

> . . . with this book . . . [the reader] may be able at once to form a just conception both of our city and of our business, and to judge whether a visit to our establishment, or our beautiful

"City of Elms," may advance his real pecuniary interests, or afford him new gratification.

We intend always to *give each buyer the full value of his money, and then to let him decide where the special expense shall be put,* and in every way to fulfill every contract so thoroughly and so promptly, that *business* shall be a pleasure, not only to us, but to those with whom we deal.

Our facilities for the manufacturing of carriages are *to-day, greater than any other establishment in the world,* and we are constantly making new additions and improvements. Very much of our work, being done by *machinery,* is executed with a *precision and exactness* that cannot possibly be attained by hand labor. Our whole establishment is conducted not only upon an extensive scale, but with the most perfect *system:*—our work being so arranged, divided and sub-divided, that each workman devotes his whole time and capacity to doing a single thing, and incidentally to devising new ways of doing that thing simpler, better and *cheaper.*

. . . for we believe we can *safely* say, that no establishment in the country, or indeed in the *world,* can *successfully compete* with us in *quality, style,* and *price.*[1]

The index to advertisements contains the Cook Company's endorsement of the advertisers. Recommendations of other New Haven carriage companies for the Cook Company's adjustable carriage seats are also included.[2] A section entitled *New Haven in 1860: A Few Notes by a Business Man Who Loves the Town* contains a description extolling New Haven's virtues.

New Haven is also a city of large manufacturing interests. It is, indeed, the chief seat in America of the trade in Carriages. There are over sixty establishments in this city for the manufacture of carriages of different kinds. Many of them are of great extent and completeness, and turn out work justly celebrated for its elegance and substantial value wherever carriages are known. The largest and most complete in all its details and arrangements is that of Messrs. G. & D. Cook & Co., which is the largest carriage manufactory in the world, and turns out a carriage completely finished for the market every hour.

Carriages from this city are to-day rolling in all parts of the United States, in Mexico, the West Indies, in Central and South America. It is rapidly coming to be felt that New Haven is to the carriage trade what Nantucket and New Bedford are to the whale fishery, Lynn to the shoe trade, and Lowell and Manchester to the trade in cotton goods; so that no dealer can now afford to depend upon any other place for his larger supplies.[3]

At the end of the catalogue is a section entitled *Carriage Manufacturing* which summarizes the advantages of doing business with G. & D. Cook & Co.:

. . . this factory is now divided into twenty-four separate departments, covering everything appertaining to the making and shipping of a carriage, each department being under the control of a competent foreman.

Following this endorsement of the principle of division of labor the courtesy with which customers are received at the Cook factory is stressed.

And should you be unable to find among the many varieties of their manufacture (which number not less than fifty) a carriage just suited to your taste, they will take you in their carriage from shop to shop, among their brother carriage-makers, until you have found the style you seek.[4]

This catalogue, while essentially a sales promotion device, provides with its advertisements and articles an overall view of the New Haven business community in the middle of the century.

The *Lawrence, Bradley & Pardee, Illustrated Catalogue of Carriages, etc.* of 1862 demonstrates pride in the company in its preface:

8. Lawrence, Bradley & Pardee from Elliot's *The Attractions of New Haven*, 1869.

Having existed over half a century, we trust it will not be
deemed egotistical should some little pride for the past be
shown, while high hopes are anticipated for the future.

We are also informed that this is the firm founded in 1810 by
James Brewster, which later became, in New York City,
Brewster and Lawrence, although known as Brewster and
Collis in New Haven. After several changes in ownership the
name of Lawrence, Bradley & Pardee was adopted in 1857.
We are told of the quality of the company's workmanship.

Our aim has always been to employ the very best workmen
by the hour, instead of piecing the work out, as is customary in
almost every other Carriage Factory. Consequently there is no
excuse for the workmen slighting anything, or not doing their
work in the best possible manner. If any are incompetent, they
soon know that "their room is better than their company."[5]

This catalogue of Lawrence, Bradley & Pardee contained
approximately twice as many illustrations of carriages as
did the 1860 catalogue of G. & D. Cook & Co., but there were
only a few general business advertisements. Both catalogues
had as frontispieces full page views of their respective factories, illustrations giving a sense of the magnitude and significance of the carriage industry in New Haven.

The various catalogues issued in 1866, 1870, 1873, 1876,
1877, 1881, and 1883 by the W. & E. T. Fitch Co. illustrate the
wide range of products made in general support of the city's
carriage industry. These items include, among others, carriage springs, malleable iron castings, curry combs, mane
combs, harness snaps, pincer wrenches, plates, wear irons,
braces, steps, trace carriers, rope fasteners, breast strap
rollers, German snaps, harness and buckle loops. Some of
these items were manufactured in New Haven by the Fitch
Company using patents owned by other companies. Statements in the 1876 catalogue indicate a possible decline in the
company's fortunes:

... on the first of January, of this year, we relinquished the manufacture of "Carriage Malleables," which will explain the disparity in size between this and previous catalogues.

We insert a few cuts of Carriage Springs, as a reminder that we continue this branch of manufacture.[6]

An undated Manville, Dudley & Co. catalogue, probably issued sometime between 1870 and 1880, emphasized that the company built only first class carriages, equal to any manufactured in the United States. It pointed out that all departments were under the supervision of a member of the firm who was a practical workman. Endorsements from satisfied customers were included from such places in addition to New Haven as Ansonia, Naugatuck, Waterbury, Wolcottville, Winsted, Norwich, and Meriden. The influence of James Brewster throughout the carriage industry in New Haven is indicated in this catalogue by the statement that Manville, Dudley & Co. carriages No. 54, 55, 56, and 101 used springs made by one of Brewster's companies.[7] The firm's 1884 catalogue offered, among others, an endorsement from Hobart B. Bigelow of New Haven, the governor of Connecticut from 1881-1883. This 1884 catalogue also referred to the company's use of Brewster's springs on carriages No. 54, 55, 56, 57, 72, and 81.[8]

The catalogue of the R. O. Dorman Co. of 1876(?) stressed that the company's carriages were products of great quality and that the business had fifteen years of successful and practical experience:

... we make it a cardinal principle to turn out only those vehicles which are thoroughly finished in every respect ...

Once again Brewster's springs were employed, on Dorman carriages No. 83, 93, 95, 104 and 105.[9]

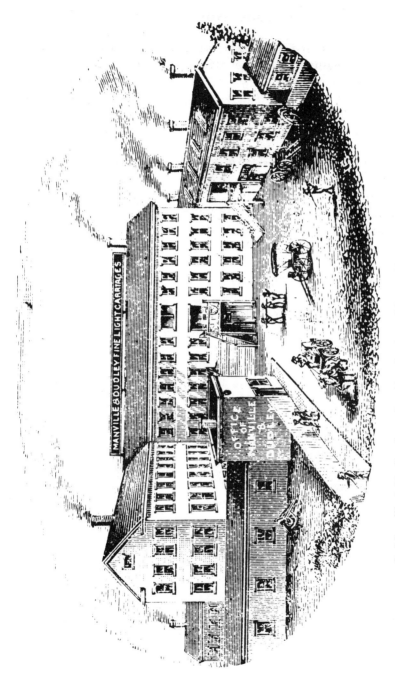

9. Manville & Dudley from *Leading Business Men of New Haven County*, 1887.

Brockett and Tuttle's catalogue of 1877(?) contained emphatic statements about the quality of the firm's products:

> Our facilities for manufacturing Carriages being unequalled, we can afford to, and do sell, first-class work cheaper than any concern in the United States.
>
> We have on hand the largest stock of fine light Carriages to be found in New England, all our own manufacture, which we cordially invite all interested in Carriages to call and examine.

Carriages No. 67, 68 and 70 had Brewster's springs.[10]

The 1879 catalogue of the Boston Buckboard Co. of New Haven featured their Murray Wagon. This had been developed by the Rev. W. H. H. Murray of Boston who, it was pointed out, was the author of *Adirondack Tales* and *Perfect Horse*. The Boston Buckboard Company derived its name from its management by a group of Boston businessmen.[11] Obviously, New Haven with its abundant supply and ready availability of raw materials, as well as workmen skilled in carriage manufacturing, attracted the attention of outsiders. The interdependence of a large segment of the New Haven carriage business is well illustrated in this catalogue by the endorsement of the Boston Buckboard Co.'s products by the following suppliers of their equipment: the New Haven Wheel Co., East Rock Axle Works, and the Mount Carmel Axle Works. The company also took pride in itself:

> . . . we shall spare no expense to make our wagons equal to any manufactured in this country.

The catalogue contained among other endorsements one from The Board of Directors of The Chicago Jockey and Trotting Club and recommendations in editorials or in articles from publications such as *Turf, Field and Farm, Spirit of the Times, Chicago Field, Live Stock Journal* and also *Daunton's Turf*.[12]

In 1880 The Dann Bros. & Co. issued a small folder describing the buckboard bodies they were manufacturing under the

patents of the J. F. Goodrich Co., another New Haven manufacturer.[13] Once again the interdependency of the local industry is illustrated. The Dann Bros. & Co. included in their
catalogue of 1881 a statement supporting their own business
and methods of operation, which included making carriage
parts for others as well as complete carriages.

> Within the memory of carriage makers now living and in ac-
> tive business, all the different parts of a carriage were made,
> put together and finished under the same roof; but the expen-
> siveness of this method gradually became apparent, and the
> manufacture of different parts—bolts, springs, axles, wheels,
> carriage parts and bodies—gradually rose into existence, each
> different branch manufacturing its own specialty and supplying
> the carriage maker with as good or better articles at less cost
> than he could produce them in his own shop.
>
> The introduction of each of these specialties met with opposi-
> tion on the part of carriage makers, but the good results ob-
> tained in their use when made by reliable manufacturers, has
> gradually overcome the prejudice against them until many of
> these auxiliary trades which furnish these specialties have
> become large and important industries, and recognized by
> carriage makers as valuable assistants in the manufacture of
> carriages.

The Dann Bros. & Co. catalogues illustrate the firm's
flexibility:

> We are also prepared to give estimates or furnish any style
> of bodies shown in the *Carriage Monthly,* of Philadelphia, or
> *Hub,* of New York . . .

The desire to export to foreign lands is also revealed:

> To those in foreign lands we would say that we have had a
> long and wide experience in furnishing our goods for export,
> through the large commission houses in New York and Boston,
> and are, to a large extent, familiar with the styles used in dif-
> ferent foreign countries.[14]

Among the company's products were dog carts, village carts, full size hearses, hearses with oval sides, and hearses with octagon sides.

While continuing in the carriage manufacturing business The Dann Brothers & Co. sought new avenues of commercial activity. The company was a specialist in bent wood products.[15] In August 1894 Clarence B. Dann obtained a patent for Demijohn Crates and in February 1896 John A. Dann secured a patent for Wheel Rims.[16] Obviously the Danns did not neglect the carriage business. Among the twentieth-century sales of automobile body parts by this ever-adapting company were those to the Pierce-Arrow Motor Car Co. of Buffalo, Fisher Closed Body of Detroit, Stevens-Duryea of Chicopee Falls, Packard Motor Co. of Detroit and the Brown and Underwood Auto Co. of New Haven. The Dann Bros. & Co. furnished materials for the construction of Peary's sledges on his expedition to the North Pole in 1909. The company advertised at the same time "Woodwork for any kind of vehicle—including AIRSHIPS—is right in our line." In December of 1921 they were selling hockey sticks to the Yale Co-operative Corporation.[17]

In 1887 G. Pierpont and Co. published a catalogue, or rather an illustrated price list, promoting their line of carriage tops, sun shades, canopy tops, and similar items. The catalogue contains the usual amount of salesmanship:

> Having made some valuable improvements in our machinery whereby we are enabled to turn out work neatly and quickly, we are better prepared than ever before to serve our customers promptly.[18]

The illustrated price list the East Rock Axle Works issued in 1887 is a typical late nineteenth-century "hard sell" publication stressing the lack of maintenance necessary for the company's product:

Always give perfect satisfaction. No sand or water can get
past the sand box . . . have been known to run one thousand
miles with one oiling.[19]

The various catalogues and price lists of A. Ochsner & Sons
dated 1889, 1892, 1894, 1896, and 1903 presented the company's line of coach and carriage locks, carriage hardware,
as well as pattern and body makers tools and similar products.
The company stressed the many years experience its work
force had:

> . . . we wish to call your attention to the fact that all our Locks
> and other goods are made from the best stock, by improved
> machinery and skilled mechanics, who have had years of expe-
> rience in the manufacturing of Locks.

Recommendations for this company's line came from such
places as New Haven, Philadelphia, Camden, Rahway, and
Newark. Emphasis was placed on these customer recommendations:

> Owing to our greatly enlarged list of patrons we refrain from
> publishing their names and letters of recommendation, as here-
> tofore, but will furnish references or copies of letters of recom-
> mendation whenever desired.[20]

A brochure of 1894 featured exclusively A. Ochsner & Son's
rotating ceiling fans, perhaps an adjustment to changing
times. From the company's several catalogues we continually
learn of its pride in its workmanship. The 1903 catalogue re-
flects optimism and adjustment to the twentieth century. It
stated that the products being manufactured were also for
automobiles and that the company's business was expanding:

> Our previously commodious quarters and large facilities for
> turning out goods have been doubled the past year. . . .[21]

The wide range of manufacturers and suppliers of supporting products to the New Haven carriage industry is well illustrated by William Perpente's catalogue of 1891 and its supplement of 1892. Featured are such items as card cases, cigar ashtrays, hand mirrors, parasol holders, handles, speaking tubes, name plates, bells, locks, tally-ho equipment, whip sockets and fasteners, and also landau top fasteners. Some of Perpente's items were manufactured by him at New Haven under patents owned by others. An examination of his catalogues and supplement seems to confirm William Perpente's confidence: "I have more new and original styles than all the rest combined. . . ."[22]

The illustrated catalogue brought out by the James Prendergast Co. in 1892 provides information on the company's various products such as carriage steps, step covers, detachable steps, coach couplings, and all-steel pole hooks. The catalogue also features files manufactured by Matthew Flanagan, Champion File Works, New Haven, once again showing the interdependence of the local industry.[23]

The catalogue of J. F. Goodrich & Co. issued in 1894(?) promoted their line of carriages and harnesses and stressed the fact they only sold carriages of their own manufacture. Their reasonable rates were mentioned and a trade-in policy was also offered. The catalogue especially solicits the custom of physicians:

> Physicians wishing to buy Carriages will save money by calling at our warerooms and examining our extensive stock. Second-hand carriages taken in trade.[24]

An undated catalogue of the Henry Hooker & Co. illustrates their extensive and varied line of carriages in what appears to be the decade before the turn of the century. Hooker company catalogues of the early twentieth century featured automobile bodies, and attempted transition.

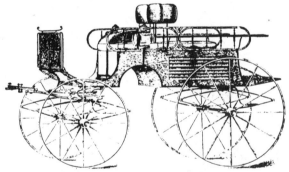
10. J. F. Goodrich & Co. and The Boston Buckboard and Carriage Co. advertisements from the *New Haven City Directory, 1891.*

HENRY HOOKER & CO., CARRIAGE FACTORY, STATE STREET.

The largest and most complete Carriage Establishment in the world.

11. Henry Hooker & Co. from *Leading Business Men of New Haven County*, 1887. A successor to G. & D. Cook & Co. Refer to figure 7, and note expansion of the factory since 1860.

The cuts of automobiles in this folder illustrate examples of our completed work in bodies. An experience in the manufacture of carriages of the highest grade for a period extending over 75 years, and in the construction of automobile bodies, for both foreign and domestic chassis, since the introduction of motor cars, warrants the assertion that our work is unexcelled as to design, construction, appointment, and durability.[25]

New Haven's carriage industry is a thing of the past, and so is the Tuttle, Morehouse and Taylor Co., the firm which printed so many of its catalogues. The industry's catalogues present by the illustrations of both products and manufacturing facilities, as well as by the various statements about the companies themselves, a method of understanding the industry's significance and contribution to New Haven. While it could be said that a distorted picture of the area's carriage industry is obtained from its "booster style" catalogues, they nevertheless convey the local feeling for and appreciation of the carriage industry in a manner similar to most such promotional material of the time.

Manuscript material pertaining to New Haven's W. & C. Dickerman & Co. confirms many previously reported patterns of development within the carriage industry. While in the section on carriage builders in Atwater's *History of The City of New Haven* W. & C. Dickerman & Co. is not mentioned, New Haven City Directories confirm that the firm existed.[26] Possibly it was too small a business for Atwater to notice. Yet a letter of December 8, 1852, from Thomas J. Finney of Vicksburg, Mississippi, supporting the fine reputation of the New Haven carriage industry, particularly desired to do business with W. & C. Dickerman & Co.

May you feel disposed to favor me with an agency and with good work and such carriages, buggies etc. as I might order and at your wholesale prices, I can give you references entirely satisfactory as to my honesty, promptness and attention to business and assurances of the immediate remittance of all my sales.

On January 10, 1853 Mr. Finney wrote again:

> If upon the receipt of this communication together with the references alluded to, you may think proper to favor me with your agency, you can notify your Natchez House of the fact after which I can confer with them upon the subject, and we may adopt any arrangements you may think best to suggest. . . . Your prompt attention and reply will much oblige.[27]

On August 3, 1854, Mr. S. Bishop of Milwaukee wrote to the New Haven company:

> I suppose you are already informed of the death of L. P. Peck, if not he expired last night after a short illness . . . and whenever the time arises that you desire an agent here to look to your interests . . . . I shall be happy to wait on you. As the first few years of a lawyers life is not fully ocupied [sic], your business would be so much clear gain to me.[28]

A letter from Robert H. May of Augusta, Georgia, dated January 20, 1855, shows worsening economic conditions in that area:

> I wrote to you some time ago to send me in Jan. this month 2 light Rockaways . . . as I have been buying from you. I am so full at present that I do not want them. I have never seen times so dull since I have been in business nor money half so hard to get. Our banks will not do any kind of paper no matter how good it is and I can't collect twenty cents on the dollar. I have owing to me nearly twenty thousand dollars that is past due ever since the first of Nov. last. What are we to do . . . .

On February 20, 1857, there is indication that Mr. May's fortunes have improved:

> Send me one more of each of those carriages like the last you shiped [sic] me finished exactly like those . . . do them up nice. I don't care how soon you ship them.[29]

Correspondence of the W. & C. Dickerman & Co. indicates the importance of the carriage manufacturing firm of G. & D. Cook & Co. as a shipping and forwarding agency for the local industry. Here once again was interdependency. Carriages were shipped from New Haven by rail and boat. Some were sent by rail to New York and then shipped by water to various coastal ports.[30]

A letter from a Mr. Watham in Charleston, South Carolina, of April 22, 1857, complained as well as made suggestions:

> I find all of your larger carriages are too small in the inside. And as I am not in want of them for some time . . . will you oblige me by having the seats made wider. There is not space enough between the front and back seats. Two persons sitting opposite are so cramped that it spoils the sale especially as the ladies wear large hoops now. If you can make them about 3 inches wider between the seats it will be the right thing.[31]

New Haven's carriage industry was not immune to events in the national labor market. A letter of March 21, 1859, from a carriage manufacturer in Newark urged the W. & C. Dickerman & Co. not to hire any striking workers that might come from New Jersey seeking employment: ". . . if you will please not employ any that may come from Rahway to get work . . . ."[32]

Another letter from Newark, dated May 11, 1861, informs the company of general conditions in the South: "Our news from N. Orleans is quite discouraging. . . ." A communication of May 24, 1861, from Mr. E. B. Dickerman in the Midwest indicates deteriorating economic conditions there. "The currency is in a bad fix. The bottom . . . has dropped out in Illinois. . . ."[33] Both letters were written after the firing on Fort Sumter.

The interest of the W. & C. Dickerman & Co. in the Southern trade is shown by their pre-Civil War shipments and by shipments to New Orleans in September of 1863 and in April of 1864—New Orleans had fallen to the Union in May, 1862. It perhaps is a surprise, this North-South trade during the war. A telegram of February 24, 1867, from R. Marsh Denman of New Orleans requesting immediate shipment of three carriages indicates some measure of success in restoring Southern trade.[34]

A letter of December 31, 1868, from George J. Underwood of New York, Commission Merchant and Dealer in General Merchandise, indicates a continuing interest by brokers in W. & C. Dickerman & Co.: "Please send us by return mail catalogue of Carriages Manufactured by You. Your early favor will oblige." The continuing existence of the South American trade in the post-Civil War period is shown by the following communication dated Nov. 11, 1869, from Samuel Lawrence & Son of New York: "If you issue a catalogue of your carriages will you please send us one with the wholesale price on each carriage. We have inquiry from Chili [sic] S.A. for the same."[35]

The Decline
of the New Haven
Carriage Industry   VI

Rollin G. Osterweis in his *Three Centuries of New Haven,
1638-1938* confirms the general opinion that the great period
of the New Haven carriage industry came prior to the Civil
War.

> So far as New Haven was concerned, its heyday of carriage-
> building ran from 1830 to 1861; the war brought serious losses
> to those manufacturers who were unable to collect their out-
> standing accounts in the Confederacy; and the economic ruin of
> the South by 1865, destroyed their principal market.[1]

In his *History of The City of New Haven* published in 1887
Edward E. Atwater described the zenith and twilight of the
New Haven carriage industry as he understood it.

> The brightest period of carriage-building in New Haven was
> from 1840 to the breaking out of the war in 1861. During this
> time New Haven carriage-makers had established a large trade
> throughout the Southern States. The war not only obliterated
> this trade, but caused very serious losses to the manufacturers
> in the obligations then due and maturing. Since that time a
> number of large firms have passed out of the carriage business,

and their factories are either used to-day for other purposes, or are standing idle, while other establishments have been enlarged and expanded on every side.[2]

The Chamber of Commerce of New Haven contended that ten years after the period about which Atwater had written the carriage industry had been seriously affected by the Civil War.

As late as 1861 [New Haven's] industries, though important, were limited in kind. Carriage making and its accessory lines were by far the largest, though the manufacture of clocks, locks, shirts and rubber boots and shoes was also carried on in a large way.

The breaking out of the civil war during this year utterly prostrated those industries for a time, and seemed likely to permanently destroy them; especially was this true of those relating to carriages, which, having southern connections to a a large extent, lost heavily. In the end, however, the war proved a blessing in at least one particular. It had the good effect of diversifying the industries of New Haven. Within a very few years afterwards many manufacturers new to the city were established within its boundaries, and were in active and prosperous operation.[3]

Emphasizing the decline of the carriage industry after the war is the statement made by Walter Allen in 1899:

Before the Civil War manufacturing industries were limited to a few lines. The most extensive of all was that of making carriages. New Haven carriages were known in every American City, and many were sent to other countries. This industry was seriously crippled by the war, owing to the large credits extended to the South; and it has never recovered its former primacy, altho [sic] still important.[4]

After the opening of the railroad from New York in the 1840s the New York and New Haven Railroad established a

12. The Henry Killam Co., Ca. 1880 [From the collection of Mr. and Mrs. William W. Gaines].

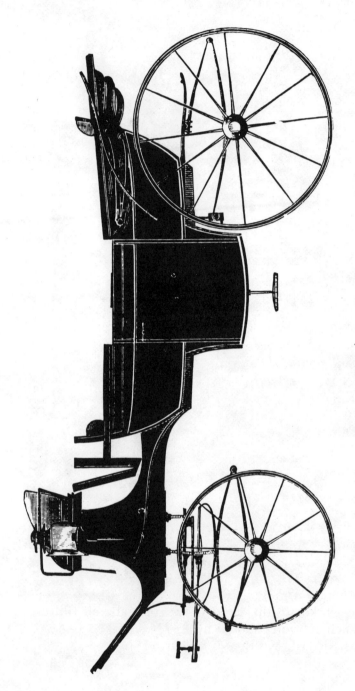

13. A Landau made by the Henry Killam Co. from *Leading Business Men of New Haven County*, 1887.

car shop at New Haven. Initially only repair work was performed there, on rolling stock belonging to the road. In 1870 the construction of locomotives and cars began. After the New York and New Haven Railroad consolidation with other railroads the amount of work done in the car shop substantially increased.[5] As a method of transportation the railroads in general were rapidly expanding, another harbinger of decline for the city's carriage industry. When the Carriage Builder's National Association was founded in 1872 only one of the forty-two founders was from New Haven.[6]

Norris Galpin Osborn places the height of prosperity for Connecticut's carriage industry as a whole in the years between 1860 and 1890. He reports that in 1860, of the 216 manufacturing establishments at New Haven approximately fifty were manufacturers of carriages.[7] New Haven carriage manufacturing, representing the largest concentration of carriage manufacturers in the country, clearly had dominated the local pre-Civil War industrial scene.

At the Centennial Exhibition of 1876 in Philadelphia the New Haven carriage industry was suitably represented. Henry Killam of New Haven was a member of the nine-man committee that co-ordinated plans for the display of American carriages. The state of the local industry was reported to be healthy:

> New Haven, Ct., with its 35 carriage shops (big and little), and a yearly production of 6000 or more vehicles, has exerted a very marked influence on the styles of American carriages, as its productions have been sold to all parts of the United States and widely copied.[8]

The exhibit of the Henry Killam Co. produced a favorable comment in the judges' report: "An important exhibit of excellent workmanship, good in design and well finished." The French cabriolet shown by B. Manville & Co. of New Haven was described as the finest cabriolet in the Exhibition.[9]

George T. Newhall closed his business in 1872. He had suffered severe financial reverses chiefly because of money owed him by southern accounts at the time of the Civil War. Nevertheless he opened a new carriage manufacturing business at New Haven in 1880 and once again prospered.[10] Shortly thereafter, in 1882, there was assurance that the local industry's reputation was still outstanding and business in general still good.

> No city in the Union has anything like the reputation that New Haven enjoys for the excellence of its Carriages. Every description of vehicle, from the lightest trotting Buggy to the most stately Coach, is turned out in her numerous factories in large numbers and in every style and finish.[11]

The *American Carriage Directory* in 1886 informed its readers that areas other than New Haven were prominent carriage producing centers: "It has been said that no city in America has had so great a development in the carriage building enterprise as Cincinnati." The directory also stated that in the post-Civil War period Mr. Lowe Emerson of Cincinnati had determined that machinery could produce interchangeable carriage parts. The previous New Haven practice and use of interchangeable parts in the manufacture of carriages was not alluded to.

> He [Emerson] came to the conclusion that carriage parts could be made by machinery, interchangeable and susceptible to duplication, as were watches, sewing machines and fire arms.[12]

Yet New Haven's reputation was not overlooked. The reader was informed that the carriage factory of Henry Hooker & Co. at New Haven was immense and its trade worldwide. In discussing the Hooker company it was mentioned that in 1874 the company's carriage business had become confined to the

B. MANVILLE & CO.,

20, 22, 24, 26

Wooster St.,

MANUFACTURERS OF

FINE FAMILY CARRIAGES,

CONSISTING OF

Four and Six-Seat Rockaways, Bretts, Victorias, Coupes, Park Phaetons, Cabriolets, Barouches, etc.

We use the Best of Material throughout, and make only First-Class Work.

New Haven, Conn.

New Haven, Conn.

N. B.—Send for Illustrated Catalogue.

14. B. Manville & Co. advertisement from *Benham's New Haven City Directory, 1874-1875.*

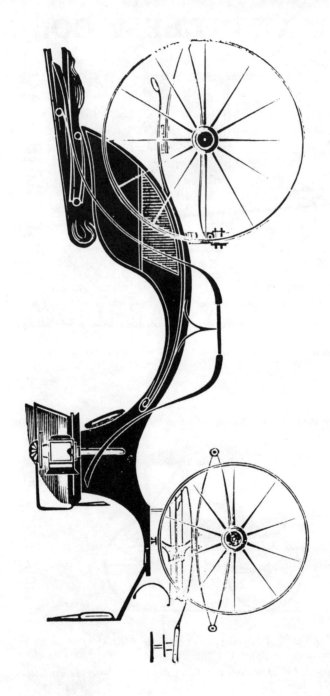

15. A Victoria made by B. Manville & Co. from *Leading Business Men of New Haven County*, 1887.

southern states, but was subsequently again expanded to other areas. The directory also reported that at the 1885 Annual Convention of the Carriage Builder's National Association at Boston a Mr. Shepard of New Haven stated that the reason New Haven workingmen were short of money with which to buy goods was that they squandered their money on "drink." He told the Association that New Haven workers spent a total of $4,000 a day at bars for alcoholic beverages.[13] (Fortunately James Brewster, having died two decades previously, was not in the audience.)

In 1885 Allerton and Stevens of New Haven produced a steam-operated fire engine. The local industry seemed to be showing some versatility.[14]

In 1888 the output of New Haven's carriage industry was reported to be worth two million dollars a year.[15] New Haven's Dann Brothers & Co. upheld the local industry's reputation by winning prizes for excellence at Melbourne, Australia, in 1888 and at Paris in 1889.[16] At the beginning of the last decade of the nineteenth century we are assured in *New Haven of To-Day* of the continuing strength of the local carriage industry:

> The most important industry of New Haven is that of carriage making, and this includes also the manufacture of all the various materials used by the carriage makers: axles, bodies, hardware, trimmings, iron-work, woodwork and wheels . . . . New Haven was the first city in America to adopt machinery in this [carriage] industry.[17]

Five New Haven carriage firms won awards in the Department of Transportation Division at the Columbian Exhibition held in Chicago in 1893. The Dann Brothers & Co. and H. G. Shepard & Sons received awards for bent woodwork. B. Manville & Co. and the New Haven Carriage Co. were awarded citations for outstanding vehicles. C. Cowles & Co. received recognition for carriage coach lamps. During the Exhibition a water color painting of the New Haven Carriage Co. factory was displayed within the Connecticut State Building.[18]

During a visit to New Haven in June 1897 of a delegation from South America, under the sponsorship of the Chamber of Commerce of New Haven, guests were given a choice of visiting one of two local industrial organizations, a corset firm or the carriage factory of Henry Hooker & Co.[19] New Haven's B. Manville & Co. had cooperated with a New York firm in providing a carriage for President Grover Cleveland.[20] The importance of New Haven as a leading center of carriage manufacturing is emphasized in an 1899 publication of the Trades Council of New Haven.[21]

Nevertheless, the center of the carriage industry was drifting slowly toward the West as the agricultural center of the country shifted. By 1900 60 percent of the country's carriages were manufactured in Indiana, Michigan, and Ohio, and 50 percent of the farm wagons were made in Illinois, Indiana, Michigan, and Wisconsin. The industry was moving toward the central states where land was cheaper, suitable lumber abundant, and where developing railroad systems provided ample transportation.[22]

In 1918 Everett G. Hill wrote of the seeming continuing strength of the local carriage industry:

> . . . despite the supposed decline in the use of the horse in the large centers of the east, New Haven has today thirty concerns rated as carriage makers.
>
> Hardly any business has so changed from its early form as that of carriage building. The horse may have diminished in numbers in New Haven, but still New Haven makes carriages for the country. The thirty carriage makers of the city are not all of them building mostly coaches for fours, and the stately landaulet gives place to more sprightly modern designs. But still there are coaches in use, and some of the finest of them are are made and trimmed here.

Hill continued his role of the commercial "historian" promoting his locality by telling of the adjustment by a segment of the city's carriage industry to the coming of the automobile.

> . . . and the D. W. Baldwin firm still builds as well as repairs carriages and automobile bodies, regardless of whether horses have any connection with them. C. Cowles & Company, a firm now well advanced in its fourth quarter of a century, makes, as it has done for years, the finest sort of coach and carriage and automobile fittings and lamps.[23]

The New Haven Carriage Co., one of the last of the large local carriage concerns, was liquidated in 1924. It attempted to adjust to the automobile industry but was only successful in manufacturing accessories. The company had been sold to the Electric Vehicle Co. of Hartford in 1900. The electric vehicle concept was unsuccessful and the company returned to the manufacture of carriages, building its last carriage in 1907. The New Haven Carriage Co. manufactured automobile bodies, notably for chassis of foreign manufacture shipped in from abroad, but this business also declined, with the shift of automobile assembling to other areas of the country. It is pleasant to report that the company passed into industrial history with ample capital, no indebtedness, real property unencumbered, and a good stock of materials: ". . . they had an allotted time and then dropped out of line like human beings."[24]

The New Haven carriage industry had as a builder of vehicles a survival in the making of basket carts, go-carts, and baby carriages, a somewhat dismal finale. The present-day automobile industry is, of course, situated in areas far distant from New Haven.

> . . . a thousand miles to the west, in a land that was still an unchartered wilderness long after Connecticut carriages were being exported to foreign countries, the great automobile industry has become localized.[25]

C. Cowles & Co., founded in 1838 as Cornwell & Cowles, later became Judson, Cornwell & Cowles and then once again Cornwell & Cowles. In 1855 it was incorporated as C. Cowles & Co. Its line of manufacture was carriage hardware, with a specialty being carriage lamps; it also produced trimmings for baby carriages. The company was well represented at the Philadelphia Centennial Exhibition of 1876.[26] Its 1938 catalog portrays the company's historical shift from carriage to motor vehicle body hardware. Door handles, door locks, interior handles, dome lamps and similar products are listed.[27] The company is New Haven's lone significant survivor of the local carriage industry. In 1971 it was known among other things for its production of rolled shapes and mouldings, stampings, stamped assemblies, and precision molded plastics.[28]

In New Haven's Wooster Square area stand visible symbols of the nineteenth-century carriage industry's prosperity. Oliver B. North had opened a plant at New Haven during the mid-century. He was one of the city's leading industrialists specializing in the making of malleable iron and hardware for the carriage industry. About 1865 he had an imposing Italian Villa style house designed for him by the well-known architect Henry Austin. This house stands today at 604 Chapel St. and has recently been restored. It bears the plaque of the New Haven Preservation Trust designating the house "A New Haven Landmark." The William Dann House, a substantial brick town house associated with the carriage company of the same name, is at 245 Greene Street in the Wooster Square area.[29] The houses are among the last reminders of a once prosperous industry, masonry and stucco monuments to an age now gone.

At one time New Haven was the leading carriage manufacturing center of the world. But in general the industry lacked the foresight to adapt to changing conditions.

No New Havener of the waning nineteenth century had vision to discern the coming of the automobile age which sent the carriage industry here into oblivion. New Haven which had the best chance of achieving the fame which finally crowned Detroit in far-away Michigan, did not adapt itself to change, and the carriage factories melted away like ice on a sultry day.

The New Haven city directory of 1900 contained for the first time the word "automobile." The fall of New Haven's carriage industry was as sudden as it was complete.[30] Some give credit to the bicycle and to the trolleys as well as the automobile.[31] The industry died primarily because New Haven did not or could not adapt its facilities to the new means of ground transportation. Possibly it could not or did not have the opportunity, for the center of the carriage industry had already shifted westward to a very considerable degree.

Epilogue   VII

A significant description of New Haven's nineteenth-century carriage industry history is given in a paragraph published in 1869 in *The Attractions of New Haven*.

> New Haven Carriage Makers, one after another, have arisen, had their day, and retired. It has been and still is to a considerable extent, a business of great importance in New Haven. It was said that during the darkest days of the war, SIXTY carriage houses closed their works in the city, and some closed probably forever. But many have been resuscitated, and have reopened largely their enterprises.[1]

Three decades later, in 1898, in *Institutions and Features of the City of New Haven,* there appeared another statement encompassing a more complete survey of the industry.

> Up to 1861 the industries of the city, while important, were limited. Carriage making headed the list . . . .
> When the Civil War broke out . . . [the] carriage industry, with its Southern connections, lost heavily. When peace came the city took on a new lease of life and its industries became more diversified.

But this industry of late years has been largely curtailed. All styles and sizes of vehicles are made here.

Factories accessory to carriage making abound and when business is good these employ large forces of men.[2]

At the turn of the century an article in the *New Haven Register* describing the state coach built by the Henry Killam Company in 1900 for the Republic of Equador also provided a reflective comment on the city's carriage industry.

> Forty years ago hardly a city of its size was better known throughout this country, through South America and abroad than New Haven. Its prominence was due to Yale College and its carriage industry. New Haven was the cradle of the carriage industry of this country.[3]

Twentieth-century commercial histories of Connecticut such as *Burpee's The Story of Connecticut* and the *History of Connecticut* by Harold J. Bingham stress the importance to the area in the nineteenth century of carriage manufacturing.[4] Well into the twentieth century, to repeat, the manufacture of carriages continued to play a part in the industrial life of the city. In the *New Haven Week Celebration* program of September 1912 we find "carriages and automobile bodies" listed among the manufactured products of the city. In the same year the Chamber of Commerce of New Haven publication, *Points of Interest,* carried an identical statement.[5]

The myth survives that the Fisher Body Division of the General Motors Corporation descended from a New Haven carriage company. This is not true. The myth came about in various ways. James Logie, who had been employed as a carriage bodymaker by New Haven's Dann Brothers & Co., moved to Chicago in 1891 where he established the Chicago Coach & Carriage Co. This company was later sold to the already existing Fisher Body Company with the Fisher organization adopting the carriage company's trademark. Another

English & Mersick, Importers, Manufacturers and Dealers in Carriage Goods, Nos. 70, 72 and 74 Crown Street.—A house which for more than a quarter of a century has maintained a prominent place among the successful industrial enterprises of New Haven is that of Messrs. English & Mersick, importers, manufacturers and dealers in Carriage Goods, Nos. 70, 72 and 74 Crown St. This reputable firm was organized for business in 1860, and from the beginning energy and progression has characterized the management.

The premises of Messrs. English & Mersick comprise two large four-story buildings, 60x100 feet and 50x80 feet in dimensions respectively,

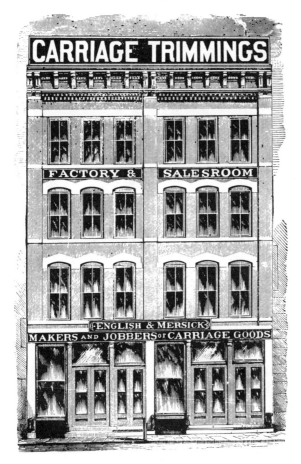

equipped throughout with improved labor-saving machinery, with a 60 horse-power engine as the motor, and from fifty to seventy-five workmen and clerks are required in the conduct of the business. The firm are among the leading wholesale dealers in and manufacturers and importers of carriage goods of every description, including the latest designs and styles of carriage hardware and trimmings for carriage builders' purposes, and the facilities of the house for supplying the most desirable merchandise at bottom prices are unsurpassed by any competitors in the United States, and carriage manufacturers throughout the country find themselves in every way advantaged by placing their orders with this old and reliable concern.

16. English & Mersick from *Leading Business Men of New Haven County,* 1887.

17. The Henry Killam Co. letter of Nov. 10, 1897. "Use all the 'pull' you have to get me a ticket for the Yale Harvard game." [From the collection of Mr. and Mrs. William W. Gaines].

possible source of the story is that William Brewster, a grandson of James Brewster, when operating Brewster & Co. in Long Island City, a successor company to James Brewster's enterprises, declined an offer to build bodies for General Motors. The Fisher Body Company later accepted such an invitation.[6]

Present-day histories on carriages give little or no attention to the New Haven industry. *Carriages* by Jacques Damase mentions the city's industry only in a vague fashion while Laszlo Tarr's *The History of the Carriage* ignores New Haven's contribution completely.[7] A major and significant segment of a world-wide industry has been essentially disregarded. Edwin Valentine Mitchell's *The Horse & Buggy Age in New England* contains a brief and uninformative biography of James Brewster and also refers to the mass production methods of G. & D. Cook & Co. *American Horse-Drawn Vehicles* by Jack D. Rittenhouse gives only a short notice to Brewster & Co. of New York and Long Island City, one of the successors of the New Haven firm.[8]

The inaccuracies and inconsistencies of city directories caution us as to their reliability, although they clearly offer a general picture of the times. These inaccuracies and inconsistencies coupled with changes in carriage company names, changes of street names, and the renumbering of the streets themselves, render impossible the preparation of a list of companies and addresses that would have any semblance of accuracy or usefulness. New Haven directories did not appear until 1840.[9] An earlier publication, *A Gazetteer of the States of Connecticut and Rhode Island,* reported in 1819 that there were in New Haven eight chaise and wagon makers.[10] A survey of New Haven directories from 1840 to 1900 indicates the following trends in carriage manufacturing (the various terms appear interchangeable):

1840 Carriage & Coach Manufacturers   17
1850 Carriage & Coach Manufacturers   19

18. The 1902 calendar of the Henry Killam Co. [From the collection of Mr. and Mrs. William W. Gaines].

1860 Carriage Manufacturers	51
1870 Carriage Manufacturers	35
1880 Carriage Manufacturers	33
1890 Carriage Manufacturers	40
1900 Carriage Makers	40

The decline in the industry after the Civil War is evident, but obviously no demise is indicated.[11] Of course counting the number of carriage factories as a method of evaluating the industry's well-being has its weaknesses.

Published census data up to 1840 are generally considered unreliable, and information obtained from it should be used with care. Changes in important definitions and classifications, revisions of census schedules, improperly trained census personnel, and unsatisfactory methods of taking returns all raise problems. Criticism of the 1850-1900 census publications is justified on the same grounds but to a lesser degree: the reports in these years are useful to a degree in showing quantitative trends. By the time of the preparation for publication of the 1900 census a permanent census office had been established, resulting in a more professional approach and greater accuracy about the material at hand. Naturally published works based on the census reports need to be viewed with at least as much caution as the reports themselves.[12]

In 1820 there were reported to be in New Haven twenty men, five women, and nine boys and girls employed in the manufacture of coaches, gigs, and other carriages. Sales were indicated to have been made chiefly in southern and foreign markets. Fifty years later there were said to be 648 individuals in the city occupied as car, carriage, and wagon makers.[13] In 1880 there were 588 persons engaged in similar capacities. While this conglomerate grouping defies precise categorization, at least the totals illustrate a decline in employment in the industry during the decade 1870-1880. In 1880 New Haven ranked fifth nationally in the dollar value of carriages and wagons produced (Cincinnati, New York,

Philadelphia and Chicago led the list, with St. Louis following New Haven). Measured by dollar volume the carriage industry was the fifth most important industry locally (Slaughtering was first, followed by corsets, rubber boots and shoes, and then hardware. Men's clothing followed the carriage industry). Tabulations in the 1880 census showed that there were twenty-six establishments at New Haven listed as carriage and wagon manufacturers, seventeen listed as manufacturers of carriage and wagon materials. Although the manufacturing statistics are not strictly comparable, in 1890 there were thirty-seven manufacturers of carriages and wagons, including custom work and repairing, and twenty-one manufacturers of carriage and wagon materials. Ten years later there were twenty-four manufacturers of carriages and wagons in the city and six establishments described as manufacturers of carriage and wagon materials. Connecticut ranked tenth among the states in 1900 in the value of carriages and wagons produced, with Ohio first.[14]

In April 1904 the national publication, *The Carriage Monthly*, was optimistic:

> Be that as it may, the world is bounding forward. Carriages will multiply, and the horse will never become extinct. He will more and more become the animal companion of man than his slavish servant. Broad highways, driveways and smooth streets will be filled with the dainty products of the higher conceptions of beauty on wheels, The Carriage builder of 1944 will be a prince in the handicrafts, and his workmanship will be a source of joy to thousands then instead of the hundreds to-day.[15]

As late as 1934 the *State of Connecticut Register and Manual* listed the manufacture of carriages as a principal New Haven industry, but carriages had not in fact been made in New Haven for many years.[16] While the city's carriage industry was adversely affected by the Civil War it had survived the conflict in reasonable condition and even prospered once again, but it was finally dealt a death blow by its inabil-

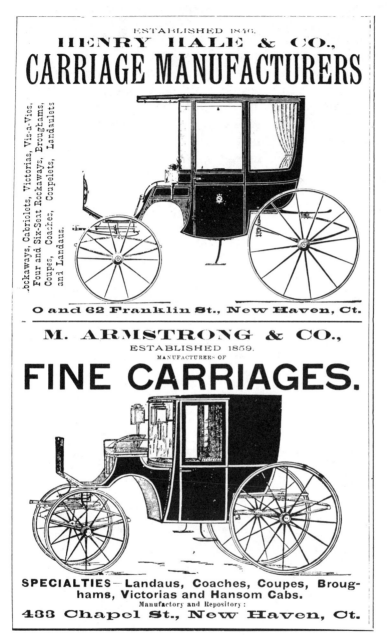

19. Henry Hale & Co. and M. Armstrong & Co. advertisements from the *New Haven City Directory, 1891.*

ity to adapt to the arrival of the automobile. New Haven
carriage companies continued to manufacture excellent
carriages while the larger carriage making centers of the middle west were turning to gasoline buggies.[17]

A coach built by the New Haven firm of Lawrence, Bradley & Pardee may be seen at the Pardee's Old Morris House
belonging to the New Haven Colony Historical Society.[18] It
is the last known surviving coach built in New Haven on
local public exhibit.

Notes

Notes to Chapter I

1. Kent T. Healy, *The Economics of Transportation in America* (New York: The Ronald Press Company, 1940), p. 3.

2. Alice Morse Earle, *Customs and Fashions in Old New England* (New York: Charles Scribner's Sons, 1893), p. 194; Douglas Waitley, *Roads of Destiny* (New York: Robert B. Luce, 1970), p. 80.

3. Rollin G. Osterweis, *Three Centuries of New Haven, 1638-1938* (New Haven: Yale University Press, 1953), p. 101.

4. Edward E. Atwater (ed.), *History of The City of New Haven* (New York: W. W. Munsell, 1887), pp. 352-355; Alice Fleming, *Highways into History* (New York: St. Martin's Press, 1971), p. 8; [U.S. Twelfth Decennial Census, 1900] *Manufacturers, Part IV* (Washington, D.C.: United States Census Office, 1902), p. 320.

5. Alice Morse Earle, *Stage-Coach and Tavern Days* (New York: The Macmillan Company, 1900), p. 271; George Francis Marlowe, *Coaching Roads of Old New England* (New York: The Macmillan Company, 1945), p. 102; Osterweis, pp. 192-193.

6. Paul H. Downing and Harrison Kinney, "Builders for the Carriage Trade," *American Heritage*, Vol. VII, No. 6, October, 1956, p. 91; Earle, *Stage Coach*, p. 313.

7. Albert S. Bolles, *Industrial History of the United States* (third edition; Norwich, Conn.: The Henry Bill Publishing Company, 1881), p. 553.

8. Wilson Flagg, *The Woods and By-Ways of New England* (Boston James R. Osgood and Company, 1872), p. xi; *A Century of Population Growth: From the First Census of the United States to the Twelfth, 1790-1900* (Washington, D.C.: Government Printing Office, 1909), p. 21.

9. Clive Day, *The Rise of Manufacturing in Connecticut, 1820-1850* (Vol. XLIV of the *Tercentenary Commission of the State of Connecticut;* New Haven: Yale University Press, 1935), pp. 8, 14, 17, 24; Fleming, p. 9.

10. Isabel S. Mitchell, *Roads and Road-Making in Colonial Connecticut* (Vol. XIV of the *Tercentenary Commission of the State of Connecticut;* New Haven: Yale University Press, 1933), p. 4.

11. Thelma M. Kistler, "The Rise of Railroads in the Connecticut River Valley," *Smith College Studies in History,* Vol. XXIII, October, 1937, pp. 11-12.

12. Percy Wells Bidwell, *Rural Economy in New England at the Beginning of the Nineteenth Century* (Vol. XX of the *Transactions of the Connecticut Academy of Arts and Sciences;* New Haven: Connecticut Academy of Arts and Sciences, 1916), pp. 312-313, 315-316; Harold Underwood Faulkner, *American Economic History* (eighth edition; New York: Harper and Row, 1960), p. 262.

13. Stewart H. Holbrook, *The Old Post Road, The Story of the Boston Post Road* (New York: McGraw-Hill Book Company, 1962), p. 212; Osterweis, p. 187; Marlowe, p. 106.

14. Edwin Valentine Mitchell, *The Horse and Buggy Age in New England* (New York: Coward-McCann, 1937), p. 16.

15. "The Rise and Development of the Carriage Building Industry in America," *The Carriage Monthly,* XL, April, 1904, 100.

16. Fleming, p. 13; Norris Galpin Osborn (ed.), *History of Connecticut* (New York: The State History Company, 1925), IV, 455; Alan Bates (comp.), *Directory of Stage Coach Services 1836* (New York: Augustus M. Kelley, 1969), introduction; Edwin Mitchell, p. 8; Osborn, IV, p. 455.

17. William Leonhard Taylor, *A Productive Monopoly* (Providence: Brown University Press, 1970), pp. 3-4.

18. Sidney Withington, *The First Twenty Years of Railroads in Connecticut* (Vol. XLV of the *Tercentenary Commission of the State of Connecticut;* New Haven: Yale University Press, 1935), p. 1; Isabel Mitchell, p. 29; John W. Barber, *History and Antiquities of New Haven, Conn.* (New Haven: L. S. Punderson and John W. Barber, 1856), p. 180; Osterweis, pp. 245-249, 362.

19. Edwin Mitchell, p. 17.

20. *History of the Post Office* (Washington, D.C.: Government Printing Office, 1968), p. 6.

21. Robert G. LeBlanc, "The Location of Manufacturing in New England in the Nineteenth Century" (Unpublished Doctoral Dissertation, The University of Minnesota, December, 1967), pp. 119, 135-136; Edwin P. Alexander, *Down at the Depot* (New York: Bramhall House, 1970), p. 9.

22. *The Carriage Monthly,* April, 1904, pp. 100-101.

23. Healy, p. 9; Blake McKelvey, *The Urbanization of America, 1860-1915* (New Brunswick, New Jersey: Rutgers University Press, 1963), pp. 75-76; Sam B. Warner Jr., *Streetcar Suburbs* (New York: Atheneum, 1972), pp. 154-155.

24. Earle, *Stage-Coach,* p. 285; John L. Weller, *The New Haven Rail-road, Its Rise and Fall* (New York: Hastings House, 1969), pp. 53-54; McKelvey, pp. 41, 79; Daniel J. Boorstin in *The Americans, The Democratic Experience* (New York: Random House, 1973) tells us that the words "street-car" and "trolley" are Americanisms.

25. Atwater, p. 370; Osterweis, pp. 335, 363.

26. "Bicycle Craze Grows in America [1892]," *The Franklin Mint History of the United States,* Franklin Center, Pennsylvania: The Franklin Mint, 1973, p. 2-3.

27. "America Enters the Horseless Age [1895]," *The Franklin Mint History of the United States,* Franklin Center, Pennsylvania: The Franklin Mint, 1973, p. 2-3.

28. Weller, p. 53; Withington, p. 31; William D. Middleton, *The Interurban Era* (Milwaukee: Kalmbach Publishing Co., 1961), p. 12.

29. Weller, pp. 56, 58; Osterweis, p. 364.

Notes to Chapter II

1. Osterweis, pp. 170-171; Carleton Beals, *Our Yankee Heritage, The Making of Greater New Haven* (New Haven: Bradley and Scoville, 1957), p. 78.

2. Beals, pp. 82-85; Atwater, p. 81.

3. Beals, p. 105.

4. Richard Shelton Kirby (ed.), *Inventors and Engineers of Old New Haven* (New Haven: New Haven Colony Historical Society, 1939), pp. 11, 22.

5. Osterweis, p. 172.

6. Thomas Rutherford Bacon, *The Hundredth Anniversary of the City of New Haven* (New Haven: General Committee on the Centennial Celebration, 1885), p. 31; Atwater, pp. 80-81; Osterweis, p. 358.

7. Osterweis, pp. 206-207.

8. LeBlanc, p. 197.

9. John Warner Barber, *Connecticut Historical Collections* (New Haven: John W. Barber, 1836), p. 100.

10. LeBlanc, p. 26.

Notes to Chapter III

1. Osborn, p. 203.

2. Atwater, p. 556; Mix's patent is not available from the Patent Office. It was probably destroyed in the 1836 fire which completely laid waste that office.

3. Barber, *History and Antiquities of New Haven*, p. 60.

4. "The George H. Durrie Diary, 1845-1846," MS in the possession of New Haven Colony Historical Society, pp. 46-47.

5. John Niven, *Connecticut for The Union* (New Haven: Yale University Press, 1965), p. 330.

6. "New Haven's Early Industries, This City Was An Important Carriage Making Center," *New Haven Register*, Sunday, December 21, 1941, p. 2, Magazine Section.

7. Timothy Dwight, *A Statistical Account of The City of New Haven, 1811*, reprint in the New Haven City Year Book, 1874, p. 32.

8. *Benham's New Haven Directory, 1860-1861* (New Haven: J. H. Benham, 1860), *passim*.

9. [U.S. Twelfth Decennial Census, 1900]*Manufactures, Part IV*, p. 306.

10. Atwater, pp. 556-557.

11. "Wagons to Wings," *New Haven Register*, Sunday, April 12, 1942, p. 3, Magazine Section; James F. Babcock, *Address Upon the Life and Character of the Late James Brewster, Delivered Before the Merchant's Exchange, New Haven, December 19, 1866* (New Haven: Tuttle, Morehouse and Taylor, 1867), pp. 16, 19-20; Osterweis, p. 251; Waleska Bacon Evans, *A Cornerstone of 1871 Focuses a Bustling New Haven* (New Haven: New Haven Colony Historical Society, 1960), p. 7.

12. Osterweis, p. 251.

13. [McLane Report] *Documents Relative to the Manufacturers in the United States Collected and Transmitted to the House of Representatives in Compliance With a Resolution of January 19, 1832 by the Secretary of the Treasury*, House Executive Document No. 308, 22nd Congress, 1st Session (Washington, D.C.: 1833), I, 1033.

14. Arnold Guyot Dana, *New Haven's Problems* (New Haven: The Tuttle Morehouse and Taylor Co., 1937), p. 13.

15. Atwater, p. 557; LeBlanc, p. 30.

16. George Anne Daly and John J. Robrecht, *An Illustrated Handbook of Fire Apparatus* (Philadelphia: INA Corporation Archives Department, 1972), p. 98.

17. Gustavus Haussknecht, *Carriage-Spring*, Letters Patent, No. 8221, July 15, 1851; Gustavus Haussknecht, *Carriage*, Letters Patent, No. 8588, December 16, 1851; Osterweis, p. 286.

18. Carroll W. Pursell Jr., *Early Stationary Steam Engines in America* (Washington: Smithsonian Institution Press, 1969), p. vi.

19. LeBlanc, p. 151; Pursell, pp. 72-73.

20. [Woodbury Report] *Letter from the Secretary of the Treasury, Transmitting, in Obedience to a Resolution of the House of the 29th of June Last, Information in Relation to Steam-Engines, & c.*, House Document No. 21, 25th Congress, 3d Session (Washington, D.C.: 1838), pp. 65-66; Dana, p. 25.

21. Pursell, pp. 103, 132; Atwater, p. 557.

22. Osterweis, p. 258.

23. Edwin Mitchell, pp. 24-25.
24. Niven, p. 14; Osborn, p. 205; *New Haven Register,* December 21, 1941, p. 2 Magazine Section; Healy, p. 81.
25. Osterweis, p. 306.
26. Niven, pp. 12, 331; Osterweis, p. 252.
27. Clive Day, p. 13.
28. Niven, pp. 332-333, 362-363.
29. *New Haven Register,* November 13, 1861, p. 2.
30. Osterweis, pp. 351-352.
31. Atwater, p. 556.
32. Osborn, p. 206; *New Haven Register,* December 21, 1941, p. 2, Magazine Section.
33. Robert Austin Warner, *New Haven Negroes* (New Haven: Yale University Press, 1940), pp. 19-20.
34. *An Introduction to the History of Wooster Square and Its Architecture, 1825-1880* (New Haven: The New Haven Preservation Trust, 1969), pp. 4, 10, 13; Kirby, p. 10; Harris Stone, "Towers and Streets of New Haven," *AIM Newsletter* [New Haven], March 1, 1970, *passim;* Dana, pp. 12a, 12b, 12c and 41.

Notes to Chapter V

1. *G. & D. Cook & Co.'s Illustrated Catalogue of Carriages and Special Business Advertiser* (New York: Baker & Godwin, 1860), pp. 4-5.
2. Ibid., pp. 13, 32.
3. Ibid., pp. 221-222.
4. Ibid., p. 226.
5. *Lawrence, Bradley & Pardee, Illustrated Catalogue of Carriages, etc.* (New York: John W. Orr, 1862), preface.
6. *W. & E. T. Fitch, Manufacturers of Carriage Springs, etc.* (New Haven: Tuttle, Morehouse & Taylor, 1876), p. 3.
7. *Manville, Dudley & Co., Fine Light Carriages* (New Haven: Tuttle, Morehouse & Taylor, 1870-1880 (?)), reverse of title page, p. 2, *passim.*
8. *Manville & Dudley, Fashionable Light Carriages* (New Haven: Tuttle, Morehouse and Taylor, 1884), p. 3, *passim.*
9. *R. O. Dorman, Manufacturer of Fine Carriages* (New Haven: Tuttle, Morehouse and Taylor, 1876(?)), p. 1, *passim.*
10. *Brocket & Tuttle, Manufacturers of Fine Light Family Carriages* (New Haven: Punderson & Crisand, 1877 (?)), reverse of front cover, *passim.*
11. Atwater, p. 565.
12. *The Boston Buckboard Co., The Murray Wagon Catalogue* (New Haven: Tuttle, Morehouse & Taylor, 1879), reverse of front cover, pp. 7-10.

13. *The Dann Bros. & Co., The Goodrich Triple Buckboard Body* (New Haven: (?), 1880), *passim.*

14. *The Dann Bros. & Co., Illustrated Catalogue* (New Haven: Tuttle, Morehouse and Taylor, 1881), reverse of title page; *The Dann Bros. & Co., Illustrated Catalogue* (New Haven: Tuttle, Morehouse & Taylor, 1882), p. 3; *The Dann Bros. & Co., Descriptive Catalog No. 21* (New Haven: Tuttle, Morehouse & Taylor, 1889 (?)), p. 1.

15. John A. Dann, *Wood Bending Machines,* Letters Patent, No. 63,997, April 23, 1867.

16. Clarence B. Dann, *Demijohn Crates,* Letters Patent, No. 524,193, August 7, 1894; John A. Dann, *Wheel Rims,* Letters Patent, No. 555,306, February 25, 1896.

17. Dann Carriage Company Collection, New Haven Colony Historical Society, a catalogue and manuscript collection, Ledger D; *Hampton's Magazine,* January, 1910, back cover.

18. *C. Pierpont and Company, Catalogue of Carriage Tops, Sun Shades, Canopy Tops, Trimmings and Dashes* (New Haven: Tuttle, Morehouse & Taylor, 1887 (?)), p. 1.

19. *East Rock Axle Works* (New Haven: Tuttle, Morehouse & Taylor, 1887), reverse of front cover.

20. *A. Ochsner & Son, Manufacturers of Coach and Carriage Locks, etc.* (New Haven: Tuttle, Morehouse & Taylor, 1889), reverse of title page, p. 6; *A. Ochsner & Son, Manufacturers of Coach and Carriage Locks, etc.* (New Haven: Tuttle, Morehouse & Taylor, 1892), reverse of p. 21.

21. *A. Ochsner & Son, Rotating Ceiling Fans* (New Haven: (?), 1894), *passim; A. Ochsner & Son, Issue No. 4, Illustrated Catalog and Price List of Coach, Carriage, Hearse and Undertakers Wagon Locks* (New Haven: Tuttle, Morehouse & Taylor, 1896), p. 1; *A. Ochsner & Son, Issue No. 6, Illustrated Catalogue and Price List of Coach, Carriage and Automobile Locks and Hinges* (New Haven: Tuttle, Morehouse & Taylor, 1903), p. 3.

22. *William Perpente, Illustrated Catalogue and Price List of Toilet Cases and Inside Coach Mountings, also Plain and Fancy Wood Turning* (New Haven: Tuttle, Morehouse & Taylor, 1891), p. 3; *William Perpente, Supplement No. 1 to the General Catalogue of 1891.* New Haven: Tuttle, Morehouse and Taylor, 1892, *passim.*

23. *The James Pendergast Co., Manufacturer of Elm City Coach Bed Clips, Carriage Steps, Step Covers, Coach Couplings, and the Pendergast Patent Anti-Rattling Whiffletree Coupling, also the Patent Detachable Step* (New Haven: (?), 1892), *passim.*

24. *J. F. Goodrich & Co., Manufacturers of Fine Carriages and Harness* ((?): (?), 1894 (?)), p. 7, pasted on.

25. *Henry Hooker & Co., Carriage Builders* ((?): (?), 1890 (?)); *New Haven Old and New, Carriage Factories, A-E,* Vol. CXXVII, p. 67.

26. Atwater, pp. 556-576.

27. W. & C. Dickerman Collection, New Haven Colony Historical Society, a manuscript collection, Box 1.

28. Ibid., Box 2.

29. Ibid., Boxes 3, 4.

30. *Cook*, pp. 66, 142; *Rates of Wharfage at Long Wharf, New Haven* (New Haven: T. J. Stafford, 1886); Dickerman, Boxes 6, 7, 10, 11, 12.

31. Ibid., Dickerman, Box 4.

32. Ibid., Box 5.

33. Ibid.

34. Ibid., Boxes 6, 10, 11, 12.

35. Ibid., Box 7.

Notes to Chapter VI

1. Osterweis, p. 252.

2. Atwater, p. 557.

3. *The Industries of New Haven and Vicinty* [sic] (New Haven: The Chamber of Commerce of New Haven, 1897), p. 59.

4. Walter Allen, "New Haven," *New England Magazine*, June, 1899, 494.

5. Atwater, p. 576.

6. "Origin and History of the Carriage Builder's National Association," *The Carriage Monthly*, XL, April, 1904, pp. 102-106.

7. Osborn, p. 205.

8. *Draft-Book of Centennial Carriages, Displayed in Philadelphia, at the International Exhibition of 1876* (New York: Hub Publishing Company, 1876), pp. 8, 26.

9. *Souvenir of the Centennial Exhibition: or, Connecticut's Representation at Philadelphia, 1876* (Hartford: Geo. G. Curtis, 1877), pp. 147-148.

10. *Palladium* [New Haven], June 6, 1890, p. 4.

11. *Commerce, Manufacturers & Resources, of New Haven, Conn.* (New York (?): National Publishing Company, 1882), p. 14.

12. *American Carriage Directory* (New Haven: Price, Lee & Co., 1886), pp. 13-14.

13. Ibid., pp. 15-16, 23-24.

14. Daly and Robrecht, p. 101.

15. Dana, p. 13.

16. *Sarasota* [Florida] *Herald Tribune*, March 6, 1972, p. 2B.

17. *New Haven of To-Day* (New Haven: The Palladium Company, 1892), p. 48.

18. *Report of the Commissioners from Connecticut of the Columbian Exhibition of 1893 at Chicago* (Hartford: Case, Lockwood and Brainard Company, 1898), pp. 49, 105, 132.

19. *Year Book of The Chamber of Commerce of New Haven* (New Haven: The Chamber of Commerce, 1898), p. 33.

20. Herbert Ridgeway Collins, *Presidents on Wheels* (Washington, D.C.: Acropolis Books, 1971), p. 102.

21. *Illustrated History of The Trades Council of New Haven and Affiliated Unions* (New Haven: The Trades Council of New Haven, 1899), p. 45.

22. Healy, p. 81; [U.S. Twelfth Decennial Census, 1900] *Manufactures, Part IV*, p. 296.

23. Everett G. Hill, *A Modern History of New Haven and Eastern New Haven County* (New York: The S. J. Clarke Publishing Co., 1918), I, 175, 182.

24. Osborn, pp. 206-207.

25. Ibid., pp. 203, 208.

26. Atwater, p. 570; *Draft-Book*, p. 102.

27. C. *Cowles & Co., 1838-1938, Motor Vehicle Body Hardware* (New Haven: C. Cowles & Co., 1938), *passim*.

28. *Economic Profile and Industrial Directory of South Central Connecticut, 1971-1972* (New Haven: The Greater New Haven Chamber of Commerce, 1971), p. 83.

29. *The Historic Houses of Wooster Square* (New Haven: The New Haven Preservation Trust, 1969), pp. 66-67, 82-83; *A Guide to Historic Hew Haven* (New Haven: The New Haven Preservation Trust, 1971), item 33.

30. Paul H. Stevens, "Elm City Lost Chance To Be World Auto Making Center," *New Haven Register*, July 30, 1933, p. 5, Section VI.

31. "Famous Bishop Horse Shoeing Shop Passes," *New Haven Register*, January 27, 1924, p. 4.

Notes to Chapter VII

1. S. H. Elliot, *The Attractions of New Haven* (New York: N. Tibbals and Company, 1869), p. 67.

2. *Institutions and Features of the City of New Haven, Conn.* (New Haven: The New Haven Union Co., 1898), p. 12.

3. *New Haven Register*, October 21, 1900, p. 3.

4. Harold J. Bingham, *History of Connecticut* (New York: Lewis Historical Publishing Company, 1962), I, 447-479; II, 557, 602; Charles W. Burpee, *Burpee's The Story of Connecticut* (New York: The American Historical Company, 1939), II, 854.

5. *Official Program, New Haven Week Celebration, September 19th, 20th and 21st, 1912* (New Haven: The Chamber of Commerce, 1912), p. 47; *New Haven Connecticut Points of Interest* (New Haven: The Chamber of Commerce, 1912), p. 1.

6. *The Story of Fisher Body* (sixth edition; (?): General Motors Corporation, 1969), *passim*; Dann Carriage Company Collection. Letter of Arthur J. Logie to Roger L. Dann dated May 23, 1972; *New Haven City Directory, 1890* (New Haven: Price, Lee & Co., 1890), p. 309; Downing and Kinney, p. 97.

7. Jacques Damase, *Carriages*, trans. William Mitchell (New York: G. P. Putnam's Sons, 1968); Laszlo Tarr, *The History of the Carriage*, trans. Elizabeth Hoch (New York: Arco Publishing Company, 1969).

8. Edwin Mitchell, pp. 16-17, 24-25; Jack D. Rittenhouse, *American Horse-Drawn Vehicles* (New York: Bonanza Books, 1948), pp. 44-45.

9. Dorothea N. Spear, *Bibliography of American Directories Through 1860* (Worcester: American Antiquarian Society, 1961), p. 217.

10. John C. Pease and John M. Niles, *A Gazetteer of the States of Connecticut and Rhode Island* (Hartford: William S. Marsh, 1819), p. 101.

11. *Patten's New Haven Directory*, 1840 (James M. Patten); *Benham's City Directory, 1850-51* (J. H. Benham); *Benham's New Haven Directory, 1860-1861* (J. H. Benham); *Benham's New Haven City Directory, 1880* (Price, Lee & Co.); *New Haven City Directory, 1890* (Price, Lee & Co.); *New Haven Directory, 1900* (The Price & Lee Co.).

12. Meyer H. Fishbein, "The Censuses of Manufactures, 1810-1890," *National Archives Accessions*, No. 57, June, 1963 (Washington, D.C.: The National Archives, 1963), p. 1; LeBlanc, p. 10; [U.S. Twelfth Decennial Census, 1900] *Manufactures, Part IV*, pp. 293-294, 300-301.

13. *American State Papers on Finance* (Washington: Gales and Seaton, 1832-1859), IV, 52: [U.S. Ninth Decennial Census, 1870] *The Statistics of the Population of the United States* (Washington, D.C.: Government Printing Office, 1872), p. 791; [U.S. Tenth Decennial Census, 1880] *Statistics of the Population of the United States* (Washington, D.C.: Government Printing Office, 1881), p. 890.

14. [U.S. Tenth Decennial Census, 1880] *Report on the Manufactures of the United States at the Tenth Census* (Washington, D.C.: Government Printing Office, 1883), pp. xxvi-xxvii, 415; [U.S. Eleventh Decennial Census, 1890] *Report of Manufacturing Industries, Part I* (Washington, D.C.: Government Printing Office, 1895), p. 60; [U.S. Eleventh Decennial Census, 1890] *Report on Manufacturing Industries, Part II* (Washington, D.C.: Government Printing Office, 1895), p. 374; [U.S. Eleventh Decennial Census, 1890] *Compendium of the Eleventh Census, Part II* (Washington, D.C.: Government Printing Office, 1894), p. 898; [U.S. Twelfth Decennial Census, 1900] *Manufactures, Part II* (Washington, D.C.: United States Census Office, 1902), p. 96; [U.S. Twelfth Decennial Census, 1900] *Manufactures, Part IV*, p. 301; U.S. Bureau of the Census, *Historical Statistics of the United States, Colonial Times to 1957* (Washington, D.C.: U.S. Government Printing Office, 1960), pp. 416, 420-422, 506.

15. "Forty Years From Now What?," *The Carriage Monthly*, XL, April, 1904, 200-NN.

16. *State of Connecticut Register and Manual, 1934* (Hartford: Published by the State, 1934), p. 389.

17. *Sarasota* [Florida] *Herald Tribune*, March 6, 1972, p. 2B.

18. Charlotte B. Sills, "The Early New Haven Carriage Builders Were True Craftsmen," *The Connecticut Circle*, May, 1938, 8-9.

Bibliography

Account of the Golden Wedding of James and Mary Brewster, September 18, 1860. Printed at the Request of Their Children, New Haven: Thomas J. Stafford, 1860.

Alexander, Edwin P. *Down at the Depot.* New York: Bramhall House, 1970.

Allen, Walter. "New Haven," *New England Magazine,* June, 1899, 480-501.

"America Enters the Horseless Age [1895]," *The Franklin Mint History of the United States,* Franklin Center, Pennsylvania: The Franklin Mint, 1973, p. 2-3.

American Carriage Directory, New Haven: Price, Lee & Co., 1886.

American State Papers on Finance. 5 vols. Washington: Gales and Seaton, 1832-1859.

Atwater, Edward E. (ed.). *History of The City of New Haven.* New York: W. W. Munsell and Company, 1887.

Babcock, James F. *Address Upon the Life and Character of the Late James Brewster, Delivered Before the Merchants' Exchange, New Haven, December 19, 1866.* New Haven: Tuttle, Morehouse and Taylor, 1867.

Bacon, Thomas Rutherford. *The Hundredth Anniversary of the City of New Haven.* New Haven: General Committee on the Centennial Celebration, 1885.

Barber, John Warner. *Connecticut Historical Collections.* New Haven: John W. Barber, 1836.

Barber, John W. *History and Antiquities of New Haven, Conn.* New Haven: L. S. Punderson and J. W. Barber, 1856.

Bates, Alan (comp.). *Directory of Stage Coach Services 1836.* New York: Augustus M. Kelley, 1969.

Beals, Carleton. *Our Yankee Heritage, The Making of Greater New Haven.* New Haven: Bradley and Scoville, 1957.

Benham's City Directory, 1850-51. New Haven: J. H. Benham, 1850.

Benham's New Haven Directory, 1860-1861. New Haven: J. H. Benham, 1860.

Benham's New Haven Directory, 1870-1871. New Haven: J. H. Benham, 1870.

Benham's New Haven City Directory, 1874-1875. New Haven: J. H. Benham, 1874.

Benham's New Haven City Directory, 1880. New Haven: Price Lee & Co., 1880.

"Bicycle Craze Grows in America [1892]," *The Franklin Mint History of the United States,* Franklin Center, Pennsylvania: The Franklin Mint, 1973, p. 2-3.

Bidwell, Percy Wells. *Rural Economy in New England at the Beginning of the Nineteenth Century.* Vol. XX of the *Transactions of the Connecticut Academy of Arts and Sciences.* New Haven: Connecticut Academy of Arts and Sciences, 1916.

Bingham, Harold J. *History of Connecticut.* 4 vols. New York: Lewis Historical Publishing Company, 1962.

Blake, William Phipps (ed.). *A Brief Account of the Life and Patriotic Services of Jonathan Mix of New Haven Being an Autobiographical Memoir.* New Haven: Tuttle, Morehouse and Taylor, 1886.

Bolles, Albert S. *Industrial History of the United States.* Third edition. Norwich, Conn.: The Henry Bill Publishing Company, 1881.

Boorstin, Daniel J. *The Americans, The Democratic Experience.* New York: Random House, 1973.

The Boston Buckboard Co., The Murray Wagon Catalogue. New Haven: Tuttle, Morehouse & Taylor, 1879.

Brewster, James. *An Address Delivered at Brewster's Hall, on Wednesday Evening, Jan. 28, 1857, to the Young Men of New Haven, Ct.* New York: Isaac J. Oliver, 1857.

Brockett & Tuttle, Manufacturers of Fine Light Family Carriages. New Haven: Punderson & Crisand, 1877 (?).

Burpee, Charles W. *Burpee's The Story of Connecticut.* 4 vols. New York: The American Historical Company, 1939.

The Carriage Monthly, April, 1904.

A Century of Population Growth: From the First Census of the United States to the Twelfth, 1790-1900. Washington, D.C. Government Printing Office, 1909.

Collins, Herbert Ridgeway. *Presidents on Wheels.* Washington, D.C.: Acropolis Books, 1971.

Commerce, Manufacturers & Resources, of New Haven, Conn. New York (?): National Publishing Company, 1882.

Connecticut Journal, July 23, 1794, p. 3.

G. & D. Cook & Co.'s Illustrated Catalogue of Carriages and Special Business Advertiser. New York: Baker & Godwin, 1860.

C. Cowles & Co., 1838-1938, Motor Vehicle Body Hardware. New Haven: C. Cowles & Co., 1938.

The Daily Herald [New Haven], September 9, 1835, p. 2.

Daly, George Anne, and John J. Robrecht. *An Illustrated Handbook of Fire Apparatus.* Philadelphia: INA Corporation Archives Department, 1972.

Damase, Jacques, *Carriages,* Trans. William Mitchell. New York: G. P. Putnam's Sons, 1968.

Dana, Arnold Guyot. *New Haven's Problems.* New Haven: The Tuttle Morehouse and Taylor Co., 1937.

The Dann Bros. & Co., The Goodrich Triple Buckboard Body. New Haven: (?), 1880.

The Dann Bros. & Co., Illustrated Catalogue. New Haven: Tuttle, Morehouse and Taylor, 1881.

The Dann Bros. & Co., Illustrated Catalogue. New Haven: Tuttle, Morehouse and Taylor, 1882.

The Dann Bros. & Co., Descriptive Catalogue No. 21. New Haven: Tuttle, Morehouse & Taylor, 1889(?).

Dann Carriage Company Collection. New Haven Colony Historical Society, New Haven, Connecticut. A catalogue and manuscript collection.

Dann, Clarence B. *Demijohn Crates.* Letters Patent, No. 524,193, August 7, 1894.

Dann, John A. *Wheel Rims.* Letters Patent, No. 555,306, February 25, 1896.

Dann, John A. *Wood Bending Machines.* Letters Patent, No. 63,997, April 23, 1867.

Day, Clive. *The Rise of Manufacturing in Connecticut, 1820-1850.* Vol. XLIV of the *Tercentenary Commission of the State of Connecticut.* New Haven: Yale University Press, 1935.

W. & C. Dickerman Collection. New Haven Colony Historical Society, New Haven, Connecticut. A manuscript collection.

BOX NUMBER

1	Correspondence: 1840-1853
2	Correspondence: 1854
3	Correspondence: 1855-1856
4	Correspondence: 1857-1858
5	Correspondence: 1859-1862
6	Correspondence: 1863-1867
7	Correspondence: 1868-1880 and also undated
8	Bills, etc., 1840-1854
9	Bills, etc., 1855-1858
10	Bills, etc., 1859-1860
11	Bills, etc., 1861-1864
12	Bills, etc., 1865-1868
13	Bills, etc., 1869-1873
14	Bills, etc., 1874-1888 and also undated

R. O. Dorman, Manufacturer of Fine Carriages. New Haven: Tuttle, Morehouse and Taylor, 1876(?).

Downing, Paul H., and Harrison Kinney. "Builders for the Carriage Trade," *American Heritage*, Vol. VII, No. 6, October, 1956, pp. 90-97.

Draft-Book of Centennial Carriages, Displayed in Philadelphia at the International Exhibition of 1876. New York: Hub Publishing Company, 1876.

Dubester, Henry J. (comp.) *Catalog of United States Census Publications, 1790-1945.* Washington, D.C.: U.S. Government Printing Office, 1950.

"The George H. Durrie Diary, 1845-1846." MS in the possession of New Haven Colony Historical Society, New Haven, Connecticut.

Dwight, Timothy. *A Statistical Account of The City of New Haven, 1811.* Reprint in the New Haven City Year Book, 1874.

Earle, Alice Morse. *Customs and Fashions in Old New England.* New York: Charles Scribner's Sons, 1893.

Earle, Alice Morse. *Stage-Coach and Tavern Days.* New York: The Macmillan Company, 1900.

East Rock Axle Works. New Haven: Tuttle, Morehouse & Taylor, 1887.

Economic Profile and Industrial Directory of South Central Connecticut, 1971-1972. New Haven: The Greater New Haven Chamber of Commerce, 1971.

Elliot, S. H. *The Attractions of New Haven.* New York: N. Tibbals & Co., 1869.

Evans, Waleska Bacon. *A Cornerstone of 1871 Focuses a Bustling New Haven.* New Haven: New Haven Colony Historical Society, 1960.

"Famous Bishop Horse Shoeing Shop Passes," *New Haven Register,* January 27, 1924, pp. 4-5.

Faulkner, Harold Underwood. *American Economic History.* Eighth edition. New York: Harper and Row, 1960.

Fishbein, Meyer H. "The Censuses of Manufactures, 1810-1890." *National Archives Accessions.* No. 57. June, 1963, Washington, D.C.: The National Archives, 1963, pp. 1-20.

W. & E. T. Fitch, Descriptive & Illustrated Catalogue of Carriage Springs, etc. New Haven: Thomas J. Stafford, 1866.

W. & E. T. Fitch, Descriptive and Illustrated Catalogue of Carriage Springs, etc. New Haven: Tuttle, Morehouse & Taylor, 1870.

W. & E. T. Fitch, Manufacturers of Carriage Springs, etc. New Haven: Tuttle, Morehouse & Taylor, 1873.

W. & E. T. Fitch, Manufacturers of Carriage Springs, etc. New Haven: Tuttle, Morehouse & Taylor, 1876.

W. & E. T. Fitch, Manufacturers of Carriage Springs, etc. New Haven: Tuttle, Morehouse & Taylor, 1877.

W. & E. T. Fitch, Manufacturers of Carriage Springs, etc. New Haven: Tuttle, Morehouse & Taylor, 1881.

W. & E. T. Fitch, Manufacturers of Carriage Springs, etc. New Haven: Tuttle, Morehouse & Taylor, 1883.

Flagg, Wilson, *The Woods and By-Ways of New England.* Boston: James R. Osgood and Company, 1872.

Fleming, Alice. *Highways into History.* New York: St. Martin's Press, 1971.

"Forty Years From Now What?" *The Carriage Monthly*, XL, April, 1904, p. 200-NN.

J. F. Goodrich & Co., *Manufacturers of Fine Carriages and Harness*. (?): (?), 1894(?).

A Guide to Historic New Haven. New Haven: The New Haven Preservation Trust, 1971.

Hampton's Magazine, January, 1910.

Hartley, Rachel M. *The History of Hamden, Connecticut, 1786-1959*. Hamden: The Shoe String Press, 1959.

Haussknecht, Gustavus. *Carriage*. Letters Patent, No. 8588, December 16, 1851.

Haussknecht, Gustavus. *Carriage-Spring*. Letters Patent, No. 8221, July 15, 1851.

Healy, Kent T. *The Economics of Transportation in America*. New York: The Ronald Press Co., 1940.

Henry Hooker & Co., Carriage Builders. (?): (?), 1890(?).

Hill, Everett G. *A Modern History of New Haven and Eastern New Haven County*. 2 vols. New York: The S. J. Clarke Publishing Company, 1918.

The Historic Houses of Wooster Square. New Haven: The New Haven Preservation Trust, 1969.

History of the Post Office. Washington, D.C.: Government Printing Office, 1968.

Holbrook, Stewart H. *The Old Post Road, The Story of the Boston Post Road*. New York: McGraw-Hill Book Company, 1962.

Illustrated History of The Trades Council of New Haven and Affiliated Unions. New Haven: The Trades Council of New Haven, 1899.

The Industries of New Haven and Vicinty [sic]. New Haven: The Chamber of Commerce of New Haven, 1897.

Institutions and Features of the City of New Haven, Conn. New Haven: The New Haven Union Co., 1898.

An Introduction to the History of Wooster Square and its Architecture, 1825-1880. New Haven: The New Haven Preservation Trust, 1969.

The 1902 Henry Killam Company Calendar.

Kirby, Richard Shelton (ed.). *Inventors and Engineers of Old New Haven*. New Haven: New Haven Colony Historical Society, 1939.

Kistler, Thelma M. "The Rise of Railroads in the Connecticut River Valley," *Smith College Studies in History*, Vol. XXIII, October, 1937, pp. 1-289.

Lawrence, Bradley & Pardee, Illustrated Catalogue of Carriages, etc. New York: John W. Orr, 1862.

LeBlanc, Robert G. "The Location of Manufacturing in New England in the Nineteenth Century." Unpublished Doctoral Dissertation, The University of Minnesota, December, 1967.

Leading Business Men of New Haven County. Boston: Mercantile Publishing Company, 1887.

McKelvey, Blake. *The Urbanization of America, 1860-1915.* New Brunswick, New Jersey: Rutgers University Press, 1963.

[McLane Report] *Documents Relative to the Manufacturers in the United States Collected and Transmitted to the House of Representatives in Compliance With a Resolution of January 19, 1832 by the Secretary of the Treasury.* House Executive Document No. 308. 22nd Congress, 1st Session. Washington, D.C. 1833.

Manville, Dudley & Co., Fine Light Carriages. New Haven: Tuttle, Morehouse & Taylor, 1870-1880(?).

Manville & Dudley, Fashionable Light Carriages. New Haven: Tuttle, Morehouse & Taylor, 1884.

Marlowe, George Francis. *Coaching Roads of Old New England.* New York: The Macmillan Company, 1945.

Middleton, William D. *The Interurban Era.* Milwaukee: Kalmbach Publishing Co., 1961.

Mitchell, Edwin Valentine. *The Horse & Buggy Age in New England.* New York: Coward-McCann, 1937.

Mitchell, Isabel S. *Roads and Road-Making in Colonial Connecticut.* Vol. XIV of the *Tercentenary Commission of the State of Connecticut.* New Haven: Yale University Press, 1933.

New Haven City Directory, 1890. New Haven: Price, Lee & Co., 1890.

New Haven City Directory, 1891. New Haven: The Price and Lee Co., 1891.

New Haven Connecticut Points of Interest. New Haven: The Chamber of Commerce, 1912.

New Haven, Connecticut: *Records of the Registrar of Vital Statistics*, Vol. 5, p. 68.

New Haven Directory, 1900. New Haven: The Price & Lee Co., 1900.

New Haven of To-Day. New Haven: The Palladium Company, 1892.

New Haven Old and New, Carriage Factories, A-E. Vol. CXXVII. New Haven Colony Historical Society, New Haven, Connecticut. A scrapbook collection.

New Haven Register, November 13, 1861, p. 2.

New Haven Register, October 21, 1900. p. 3.

New Haven Register, May 31, 1902, p. 2.

"New Haven's Early Industries, This City Was An Important Carriage Making Center," *New Haven Register,* Sunday, December 21, 1941, p. 2, Magazine Section.

Niven, John. *Connecticut for The Union.* New Haven: Yale University Press, 1965.

A. Ochsner & Son, Manufacturers of Coach and Carriage Locks, etc. New Haven: Tuttle, Morehouse & Taylor, 1889.

A. Ochsner & Son, Manufacturers of Coach· and Carriage Locks, etc. New Haven: Tuttle, Morehouse & Taylor, 1892.

A. Ochsner & Son, Rotating Ceiling Fans, New Haven: (?), 1894.

A. Ochsner & Son, Issue No. 4. Illustrated Catalogue and Price List of Coach, Carriage, Hearse and Undertakers' Wagon Locks. New Haven: Tuttle, Morehouse & Taylor, 1896.

A. Ochsner & Son, Issue No. 6. Illustrated Catalogue and Price List of Coach, Carriage and Automobile Locks and Hinges. New Haven: Tuttle, Morehouse & Taylor, 1903.

Official Program, New Haven Week Celebration, September 19th 20th and 21st, 1912. New Haven: The Chamber of Commerce, 1912.

"Origin and History of the Carriage Builder's National Association," *The Carriage Monthly,* XL, April, 1904, 102-106.

Osborn, Norris Galpin (ed.). *History of Connecticut.* 5 vols. New York: The State History Company, 1925.

Osterweis, Rollin G. *Three Centuries of New Haven, 1638-1938.* New Haven: Yale University Press, 1953.

Palladium [New Haven], March 7, 1860, p. 3.

Palladium [New Haven], June 6, 1890, p. 4.

Patten's New Haven Directory, 1840. New Haven: James M. Patten, 1840.

Pease, John C., and John M. Niles. *A Gazetteer of the States of Connecticut and Rhode Island.* Hartford, William S. Marsh, 1819.

The James Pendergast Co., Manufacturer of Elm ₌City Coach Bed Clips, Carriage Steps, Step Covers, Coach Couplings, and the Pendergast Patent Anti-Rattling Whiffletree Coupling, also the Patent Detachable Step. New Haven: (?), 1892.

William Perpente, Illustrated Catalogue and Price List of Toilet Cases and Inside Coach Mountings, also Plain and Fancy Wood Turning. New Haven: Tuttle, Morehouse & Taylor, 1891.

William Perpente, Supplement No. 1 to the General Catalogue of 1891. New Haven: Tuttle, Morehouse and Taylor, 1892.

C. Pierpont and Company, Catalogue of Carriage Tops, Sun Shades, Canopy Tops, Trimmings and Dashes. New Haven: Tuttle, Morehouse & Taylor, 1887(?).

Porter, William. "The Farmington Canal," *New Haven Colony Historical Society Journal,* Vol. XX, October, 1971, 49-66.

Pursell, Carroll W. Jr. *Early Stationary Steam Engines in America.* Washington: Smithsonian Institution Press, 1969.

Rates of Wharfage at Long Wharf, New Haven. New Haven: T. J. Stafford, 1866.

Report of the Commissioners from Connecticut of the Columbian Exhibition of 1893 at Chicago. Hartford: Case, Lockwood and Brainard Company, 1898.

"The Rise and Development of the Carriage Building Industry in America," *The Carriage Monthly,* XL, April, 1904, 97-101.

Rittenhouse, Jack D. *American Horse-Drawn Vehicles.* New York: Bonanza Books, 1948.

Sarasota [Florida] *Herald Tribune,* March 6, 1972, p. 2B.

Shepard, Charles U. *Outline of the Franklin Institution of New Haven.* (?): Baldwin and Treadway, (?).

Sills, Charlotte B. "The Early New Haven Carriage Builders Were True Craftsmen," *The Connecticut Circle,* May, 1938, 8-9, 53.

Souvenir of the Centennial Exhibition: or, Connecticut's Representation at Philadelphia, 1876. Hartford: Geo. G. Curtis, 1877.

Spear, Dorothea N. *Bibliography of American Directories Through 1860.* Worcester: American Antiquarian Society, 1961.

State of Connecticut Register and Manual, 1934. Hartford: Published by the State, 1934.

Stevens, Paul H. "Elm City Lost Chance To Be World Auto Making Center," *New Haven Register,* July 30, 1933. p. 5 Section VI.

Stone, Harris. "Towers and Streets of New Haven," *AIM Newsletter* [New Haven], March 1, 1970.

Storer, William. *New Haven as It Is*. New Haven: William Storer, 1845.

The Story of Fisher Body. Sixth edition. (?): General Motors Corporation, 1969.

Tarr, Laszlo. *The History of the Carriage*. Trans. Elizabeth Hoch. New York: Arco Publishing Company, 1969.

Taylor, William Leonhard. *A Productive Monopoly*. Providence: Brown University Press, 1970.

Tuttle, Morehouse & Taylor, Fifty-Five Years. New Haven: Tuttle, Morehouse & Taylor, 1914.

Alexander Catlin Twining Papers. New Haven Colony Historical Society, New Haven, Connecticut. A manuscript collection.

U.S. Census

　U.S. Bureau of the Census. *Historical Statistics of the United States, Colonial Times to 1957*. Washington, D.C.: U.S. Government Printing Office, 1960.

　[U.S. Ninth Decennial Census, 1870] *The Statistics of the Population of the United States*. Washington, D.C.: Government Printing Office, 1872.

　[U.S. Tenth Decennial Census, 1880] *Statistics of the Population of the United States*. Washington, D.C.: Government Printing Office, 1881.

　[U.S. Tenth Decennial Census, 1880] *Report on the Manufactures of the United States at the Tenth Census*. Washington, D.C.: Government Printing Office, 1883.

　[U.S. Eleventh Decennial Census, 1890] *Compendium of the Eleventh Census, Part II*. Washington, D.C.: Government Printing Office, 1894.

　[U.S. Eleventh Decennial Census, 1890] *Report of Manufacturing Industries, Part I*. Washington, D.C.: Government Printing Office, 1895.

　[U.S. Eleventh Decennial Census, 1890] *Report on Manufacturing Industries, Part II*. Washington, D.C.: Government Printing Office, 1895.

　[U.S. Twelfth Decennial Census, 1900] *Manufacturers, Part II*. Washington, D.C.: United States Census Office, 1902.

　[U.S. Twelfth Decennial Census, 1900] *Manufacturers, Part IV*. Washington, D.C.: United States Census Office, 1902.

U.S. Department of Commerce. *The Story of the United States Patent Office.* Washington, D.C.: U.S. Government Printing Office, 1972.

"Wagons to Wings," *New Haven Register,* Sunday, April 12, 1942, p. 3, Magazine Section.

Waitley, Douglas. *Roads of Destiny.* New York: Robert B. Luce, 1970.

Warner, Robert Austin. *New Haven Negroes.* New Haven: Yale University Press, 1940.

Warner, Sam B. Jr. *Streetcar Suburbs.* New York: Atheneum, 1972.

Weller, John L. *The New Haven Railroad, Its Rise and Fall.* New York: Hastings House, 1969.

West Haven, Connecticut: *Records of the Registrar of Vital Statistics,* May 29, 1902.

Withington, Sidney. *The First Twenty Years of Railroads in Connecticut.* Vol. XLV of the *Tercentenary Commission of the State of Connecticut.* New Haven: Yale University Press, 1935.

[Woodbury Report] *Letter From the Secretary of the Treasury, Transmitting, in Obedience to a Resolution of the House of the 29th of June Last, Information in Relation to Steam-Engines, & c.* House Document No. 21, 25th Congress, 3d Session. Washington, D.C. 1838.

Year Book of The Chamber of Commerce of New Haven. New Haven: The Chamber of Commerce, 1898.